Hold thy bloody hand!
Why dost thou lash that whore?
Strip thine own back;
Thou hotly lusts to use her in that kind
For which thou whipp'st her...

— *William Shakespeare's King Lear:*
Act 4 Scene 6

WHAT THE MEDIA SAID

'It's probably the best-selling book in the history of Singapore publishing, with copies at Changi Airport constantly moving off the shelf. A rather insightful and cleverly researched book that neither glamorises nor puts down the trade.' ETC

'A book (No Money, No Honey!) describing Singapore's multi-million dollar prostitution trade has become the island-republic's longest-running bestseller.' THE JAPAN TIMES

'The unofficial travel guide to Singapore's underbelly.' PERSONALITY

'The author has obviously done extensive research. What we get is a clear, guided map to Singapore's red-light districts. All questions are answered — from how much to what can be gotten.' MARIE CLAIRE

'No Money, No Honey! gives some background to prostitution in Singapore but it's the interviews that are the most riveting. Hookers in many guises — escorts, masseuses, part-timing housewives — give their reasons why they engage in something so demeaning.' HER WORLD

THE FOURTH EDITION

NO MONEY, NO HONEY!

DAVID BRAZIL

Angsana Books

SINGAPORE · KUALA LUMPUR

Published by **A** *Angsana Books*

Angsana Books is an imprint of
FLAME OF THE FOREST Pte Ltd
Yishun Industrial Park A
Blk 1003, #02-432
Singapore 768745
Tel: 65-7532071, Fax: 65-7532407
Email: angsana@pacific.net.sg

Fourth Edition Copyright © Flame Of The Forest Pte Ltd, 1998
This book has been reprinted *10* times

Cover by Mangosteen Designs
Front cover picture posed by model from Jeffrey Chung Models.

All photographs in this book are by David Brazil.

Printed in Singapore

ISBN 981-3056-16-9

For all the women who
loosened their lips (only!)
and opened their hearts (only!)
for me...

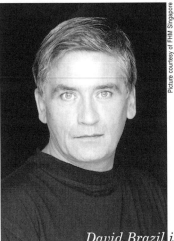

About The Author

David Brazil is a Dublin-born Londoner who came to Singapore in 1988. Now primarily a journalist/photographer, he has contributed words and pictures to most major Singapore newspapers and magazines on a wide range of topics, including travel, the meaning of life, fashion, sex, football, nightlife, local history and the potatoes in mutton curries. He has edited various publications (such as Changi Airport's magazine) and most recently, was deeply involved with FHM Singapore and ETC magazines. He played a leading role in the award-winning Mee Pok Man movie, and is an occasional TCS-TV comedy actor, male model and tourism lecturer. His ambition is to give up smoking.

CONTENTS

'No Sleaze Please, We're Singaporean!'

Prostitution has always been in Singapore. Ever and even since Stamford Raffles got the ball rolling in 1819. Before he left his Singapore for the final time in 1823, Raffles wrote: 'The unfortunate prostitute should be treated with compassion, but every obstacle should be thrown in the way of her service being a source of profit to anyone but herself.'

A realistic man, Raffles knew his bold new island enterprise would attract footloose men from all around Asia, so it would also attract women to 'service' those men — and to raise themselves out of poverty by means of what was then probably the only career opportunity open to them as women.

A compassionate man also, Raffles knew that such women would be exploited by men (and other women), and he was expressing his clear distaste for pimps who creamed their chunks off what women earned the hard way — by parting their legs for money.

By 1898, the Chinese Protectorate's records showed

that Singapore had 200 registered brothels employing over 3,000 women (mainly Cantonese), plus 150 unregistered brothels containing some 600 (mainly Teochew) women. The Chinese single male population about this time was 275,000, so little wonder that four in every five women arriving from China at Boat Quay were speedily whisked off to Chinatown's brothel zone. This became known as the Blue Triangle (bounded by today's Keong Saik Road, Teck Lim Road and Jiak Chuan Street).

Until the early 1930s, the centre of the open-to-all-races red light zone was Malay Street. But post-war, it had shifted to the Selegie-Jalan Besar-Lavender-Balestier area and Desker Road — where women during the 1950s charged the quirky rate of $5.60 (a 'five-sixty', as it became known). Following the anti 'yellow culture' clampdowns after 1959's independence, the bulk of Singapore's vice moved to Geylang where it still operates today (as, of course, does Desker Road).

And as it does in many other parts of modern Singapore. Even if many people living here don't realise it — or choose to not realise it. Many are the letters to newspapers by Singaporeans grumbling at manifestations of Singapore's sex-for-sale industry. Letters usually on the theme 'no sleaze please, we're Singaporean', letters even insisting that kind of thing happens only in Haadyai, Patpong, Batam and their ilk — not in clean, green, shoppers' paradise etc Singapore.

But it does, it always has done and it undoubtedly will continue to do. Thus this book...

No Money, No Honey! aims to give as full as possible a picture of Singapore's sex-for-sale industry. It's not an academic thesis nor a sociological survey, more a journalistic exploration.

Its centrepiece is probably the girls themselves, talking in the frank and blunt way in which they would be expected to. Talking about their actual work, rather than outlining how their psychological or sociological profiles directed them into that line of work.

Thus there are few examinations of tormented childhoods, abusive parents, nasty husbands, boyfriend-pimps, expensive habits and so on. I wanted to know the nuts and bolts of their working lives, not how or why they had made their 'career-path' decisions — because it's obvious and basic: to make money.

The first chapter looks at Singaporean men and women's attitudes towards sex-for-sale. The second examines today's sex-for-sale industry in Singapore.

Then it's the girls themselves: twelve of them involved in the various levels of sex-for-sale — from the top-of-the-line stuff to the back lane low-rent streetwalkers, and most stages in between.

That's followed by a look at the unavoidable issue of sexually transmitted diseases and the dreaded Aids.

Again, this book is not a work of fiction, nor the outpourings of an overheated erotic male imagination. This is real. This is for real. This is what is going on in certain parts of Singapore today.

If readers would rather pretend that all this just doesn't or can't happen in 'squeaky-clean' Singapore, that's their decision. What they can't — and shouldn't — do is to insist that all this isn't happening at all.

Note: Unless otherwise stated, Singapore dollars will be used.

CHAPTER I

Men and Women in Singapore's Sex-for-sale Business: It Takes Two to Tango

More than 6,000 women offer sex-for-sale in today's Singapore. This is an unofficial estimate that includes all known levels of sex-for-sale, from full-time hookers to occasional dabblers and including Thai, Indonesian, Filipina and other women here on 'working holidays'. The actual figure may well be higher.

And if 6,000-plus sounds high, consider this. In August 1998, the UN-linked International Labour Organisation published its The Sex Sector report which gave the following figures (based on 1993–94 estimates) for women working as prostitutes in South-east Asian nations. Indonesia: 140,000 to 230,000; Philippines: 500,000; Thailand: 300,000 to 400,000; Malaysia: 142,000.

The ILO insisted that the sex industry accounted for 2–14 percent of these countries' GDP (in Indonesia, ILO put the sex-for-sale annual turnover total as $6.1 billion) — and that the various governments should therefore recognise their sex industries as a valid economic sector, subject to taxation and the like.

In Singapore (as around the region), with so many women offering sex-for-sale, there is clearly a high number of local men willing to buy all this on-offer sex. For prostitution functions on classic supply and demand principles, and is as subject to market forces as any other line of service work.

Indeed, nearly half of the sexually experienced men in today's Singapore have probably had sex with a prostitute.

Probably, because this high proportion of an uncertain total figure is an extrapolation from the findings of the Survey On Partner Relations And Knowledge, Attitude, Behaviour and Practice On Aids in Singapore.

This mouthful-of-a-title, acronym-defeating survey was conducted in 1989 by the Health Ministry, National University of Singapore and World Health Organisation. It surveyed 2,115 Singaporeans (aged 15–49) over a period of three months, asking them extremely personal questions. Its findings emerged in *The Sunday Times* of May 17, 1992.

The men-and-prostitutes estimate was arrived at in the following manner. Nearly one in 10 men queried in the survey said they had engaged in 'casual sex' during the previous 12 months, mostly with prostitutes (this coming under the category heading of 'a sexual encounter with a stranger').

Subtracting from the 1-in-10-induced total those men who were still virgins, very old and other men who said they'd never had sex at all — and the proportion of sexually active Singaporean men visiting prostitutes was bumped up to 1-in-6.

Then, according to two academic researchers involved in conducting the survey, allowance had to be made for the 'honesty factor'. They suggested that the actual figure of men partaking of sex-for-sale reached nearly 50 percent of 'sexually experienced' men. It should also be pointed out that of the single men (of all age groups) queried in the survey, 25 percent said they'd never had sex at all.

But, as with all surveys, validity does depend on the honesty of responses — which for many reasons, some obvious, cannot be taken for granted when the topic is sex. So, as a cunning 'lie-detector' test in the 1989 Aids survey, nine women with a known history of prostitution were included among the women queried (they obviously did not know their sexual background was thus known by the researchers).

The result? Of these nine, two lied about their background — with one even claiming she was still a virgin!

Likewise, a group of 14 who were known to have suffered from sexually transmitted diseases were 'secretly' queried — and of this group, just one-third gave truthful responses.

Neither the prostitutes nor the ex-STD victims were included in the survey's overall findings. But they did convince the researchers that the true numbers could well be up to three times higher than the figures finally given in the survey.

Further factors influencing the belief that more men were being naughty than were prepared to personally 'own up' came from the 22 percent figure (1-in-5) of men queried who said it was 'OK' for men to visit prostitutes.

Incidentally, when these same men were asked about women having casual sex or extramarital affairs, more than 95 percent of them said it was decidedly 'not OK'.

Plus the fact that, when faced with a sample series of sexual scenarios of which men were asked to approve/disapprove, the level of permissiveness they claimed in their 'approve' ratings did not coincide with what they had reported in terms of their personal sexual behaviour.

Put simply — and bluntly — many of the men thus surveyed were not telling the truth, the whole truth and nothing but the truth about their own sexual activities.

A further survey finding (of uncertain relevance to our current purpose) was that 48 percent of men who had their first sexual encounter before they turned 21 had not (eventually) married their first sex partner, whereas of those men whose virginity went between the ages of 25 and 29, 93 percent had indeed married or were married to that first sexual partner.

Now, what did the survey find when it switched its probing to females? It found this: that virtually every Singaporean woman queried — of all age and race groups — said she had never slept with a man whom she did not/had not married.

So, what have we here? Maybe a significant proportion of these women were also being economical with the truth (through modesty, or primness?) when asked if they'd slept with a man who was not their husband, or who did not later become their husband;

that is, if they'd had casual sex.

Such a suspicion is added to by a 1990 study on the sexual behaviour of medical students. This found that 12 percent of final-year female students had partaken of premarital sex (unclear whether this meant with the men they were to marry, or not). And a 1988 survey of 1,800 teenagers by the Singapore Planned Parenthood Association revealed that five percent (1-in-20) of teenage girls did have (or had had) sex on their dates.

But if we accept the 1989 survey's finding that virtually no Singaporean women 'did' casual sex, then we have to ask this: just who were the women on the 'receiving end' of all those men who said they did have sex with women who were not (or who did not become) their wives?

Presumably, they were Singapore's sex-for-sale women. Of whom, as we have noted, there are over 6,000.

1992 proved to be a vintage year for publishing the results of personal-life local surveys. For in August, the memorable survey commissioned by the Censorship Review Committee emerged (face-to-face interviews had been conducted with 1,102 'representative' Singaporeans aged 17 and above, over a period of two months).

Overall, the conclusion was that modern Singaporeans had said a big 'no' to liberal values, defining themselves as conservative in their views on issues such as sex and marriage. Among its many fascinating individual findings were that 67 percent disapproved of premarital sex; and that 90 percent disapproved of extramarital sex.

But — and it was a big 'but' — were the respondents giving truthful answers or not?

One letter writer to *The Straits Times*' Forum page, Eddie Song Tiang Ann, clearly thought not: 'Not many people are bold enough to express their true feelings for fear of being branded as *cheeko*, *hum sup* or *buaya* (dialect terms to describe people who are sexually lively).

'If you ask someone whether he or she likes to read *Playboy* or *Playgirl* magazines, the answer is likely to be a firm "No". However, if he or she has a chance to obtain such magazines, he/she is likely to spend an hour in the toilet enjoying them.

'The *kiasu* mentality of Singaporeans is well known. They will not say anything that they think will put them in a bad light.'

Eddie Song noted, most relevantly for our current purposes, that: 'If the survey shows that 90 percent disapprove of extramarital sex, the real figure may be much lower as some respondents who "disapprove" of extramarital sex may be indulging in it secretly, if not in Singapore, then overseas.'

And: 'If you ask people in respectable occupations... whether they patronise massage parlours, their answers will inevitably be in the negative... Singapore society has an unhealthy excess of moral hypocrites and bigots!'

Enough of surveys, truthfulness thereof, responses to and the like. For all roads lead back to our central point. Which is that over 6,000 women in Singapore offer sex-for-sale.

Why do they do so? The women cover all levels,

from streetwalkers and part-time housewives to installed-in-a-nice-flat mistresses. But, what links them all of course is they all do sex for money.

Which, at the low end, means women needing cash to pay off those mounting domestic bills before they can start to think about treats for themselves. Prostitution offers probably the easiest, quickest, tax-freest way of doing so for women who didn't conquer the harsh demarcation lines of Singapore's education system or who found themselves with children to support all by themselves.

Then there are women who do it for kicks, for thrills, because their everyday life is too dull. Or those women with an activated sexuality, but who cannot give it full expression within the confines of conventional Singaporean society. Or those women at the higher end of the sex-for-sale range, who know what huge sums of money can come their way while the going is good.

And they do it in many ways...

Streetwalker girls lurk in Geylang corners.

CHAPTER 2

Sex-for-sale Today

GEYLANG

Geylang must be unique. What other big cities in the world have such a mixed-up, muddled-up red-light district? And that includes London's famously cosmopolitan Soho.

Take Lorong 12, for instance. From the Guillemard Road end, this starts off with two run-down joints which function as short-time 'knocking shops' for the streetwalkers who work this patch. Then it's a missionary society and an ornate temple. Then two more slightly better (air-con rooms, etc) 'knocking shops', then private houses mixed up with small clan or trade association (real old-style ones are located all around Geylang, such as Singapore Permanent Hair Waving Employers' Association) bases — with a smattering of pugilistic or dragon dance arts centres, ending up with Geylang Road's very relaxed coffee shops.

Back again, following the road around Geylang United football team's training ground onto Talma

Road, there's another terraced house used by (usually Indonesian) freelance girls, this one discreetly converted into eight or so bedrooms for short-time hire by male clients.

This small zone is one of the very few streetwalker areas in town, and here by day or by night men passing by may hear whispered words like 'Hello, Mister! Looking for a girl?' from the shadows or from behind parked cars or clumps of trees. Here, you often hear the girls (or the occasional *ah quah*) before you see them. Many men hang out here too, watching Geylang's skilled footballers doing their training routines or, more likely, gawking at this entertaining roadside Geylang Vice free show.

Geylang Vice proper works on a more organised, controlled basis. It reaches from Lorong 4 to Lorong 24, bounded by Guillemard and Geylang Roads, with the occasional outpost beyond Lorong 24 or between Geylang Road and Sims Avenue. It is most concentrated in the rectangle formed by Lorongs 16, 18 and 20, linked by Westerhout Road. Lorong 24, with its attached little side-streets, is also dense with bordellos. Overall, the business is so thriving that new joints are opening all the time; currently along Lorong 4, where some are now using the Thailand 'viewing room' style of displaying their girls.

Overall, there must be up to 250 brothels based in Geylang's lorongs. Some are easy to spot, especially those that occupy a whole house (terrace or fully-detached) and with enticing names such as 'Paradise'. When darkness descends, their festive fairy lights are switched on and they can even look rather jolly. Other

Geylang girls: they come, they go or they wait, dressed to thrill.

brothels are not so obvious. They could be just the one flat in an apartment block. Or a battered old bungalow. The giveaway is their number. If a house or flat number appears in big numerals, either on a light box or in a colourful, unusual style, that's a cathouse.

The larger ones often have old-men touts outside inviting likely looking males to enter and enjoy the female delights within. Such brothels are the ones pitched at the tourist trade (which means some of their girls speak at least a little English — and some Japanese, too), as well as locals. Indeed, at least two upmarket brothels presumably specialise in a Japanese clientele (going by the Japanese-style calligraphy outside, or Japanese names). The more upmarket joints can be located in very nice new town houses — further testimony to how profitable Singapore's vice business must be.

The touts happily explain the deal inside these upmarket brothels (often with friendly 'Welcome' signs, with another making great play of its house number — 69 — the shape of which numerals has an erotic connotation for Westerners). As if they were selling durians, they give their sales pitch — the deal being a 's*ck and f*ck' session for an all-in, no plus-plus, prepaid price (though tips are always appreciated by the girls, of course).

These touts even offer some useful hints. One told me: 'We're open from noon to 3 am but the best time is 6 to 10 pm when most of the girls are available and still "fresh". But by midnight, the best girls "go". Why don't you come in and inspect? You'll like what you see…'

Geylang cathouses: it's the gaudy house or flat number that gives the game away.

Which is a little misleading. Because most brothels don't have their own stable of fillies. The system is this: once a girl decides to work in Geylang, she must be 'licensed' by means of a Yellow Card (the size and style of the usual ID card). This establishes her identity, her profession (discreetly), carries her photo and a thumbprint.

Its continued possession requires that the girl visit a doctor every fortnight for a check on her sexual health. The yellow card system also means that the girl cannot do her work outside the Geylang zone, cannot do overnights or go to clients' homes, nor work freelance.

Which doesn't mean they don't get clients from the Orchard Road hotel belt or wherever. That's when taxi-drivers enter the vice picture. Many, especially those who work night shifts, know what (and where) to suggest to male passengers who ask or who just look likely. Many hotel doormen know this system too.

Some cabbies have deals with the doormen, and have deals with particular Geylang brothels, and get their cuts. These cabbies also keep an eye open for yellow card girls at work away from their Geylang patch on a freelance basis; such errant females can get 'punished' nastily by their pimps.

Whereas some of the upmarket brothels do have girls who work exclusively for them, most yellow card girls work the lorongs on a 'supply and demand' basis. That is, in response to customer bottlenecks or to specific (race, age, price etc) requests. They get phoned for, or paged by the brothel requiring their services — and it is this brothel that will pay the girl her cut from her

Geylang's streetwalker strip, where the girls try to 'outwit' regular Anti-Vice police car patrols.

National Day or Hungry Ghosts month: it's business as usual in Geylang.

labours.

Sipping a drink outside a Geylang Road coffee shop gives the opportunity to watch these female comings and goings. A constant flow of cars and taxis pull up at lorong addresses, and alluringly, sexily dressed girls get out or in — depending on whether they're off for a job or returning to base camp, mission accomplished.

And often, given that the venues are rarely spaced far apart, fully made-up and glampuss-attired (either in skimpy and clingy Spandex garb or Chinese night-club-style thigh-slit allure) girls on their own can be spotted, tottering on their trademark high heels from one joint to another. On their own without fear, because although Geylang is a sex-for-sale venue, it is also by and large a safe neighbourhood, without that chilling air of menace or nastiness found in other big-city red-light districts.

Geylang's lorongs are at their busiest on Friday and Saturday nights, during festive seasons and at year-end bonus times. They slow right down on Mondays, on days before big horse-race meets (many Chinese men fear visiting a prostitute will bring them bad luck with their bets), the Muslim fasting month (for Malay men), and during the Hungry Ghosts Seventh Month (for Chinese men).

There is no obvious evidence that Geylang's vice is controlled by any tightly organised secret societies or criminal gangs. The brothels seem to have individual owners, though there is some group collusion (such as in staking claims to particular girls). And around the lorongs there are all sorts of spin-off commercial activity — ranging from the *mamak*-stalls with their unusually large selection of condoms (alas, including some of those seven Asian brands identified as defective — that is, they leak — by the Health Ministry in 1993) to Geylang Road's many well-patronised late-night eateries. These are reputed to provide some of the best eats in Singapore.

Plus its busy small hotels and boarding houses. These crop up all around Geylang and by and large serve as short-time venues for freelance girls working Orchard Road (especially Thai Takeaways) or as cramped sleeping quarters for working girls who do not get an overnight.

In these boarding houses, there can be outbreaks of savage drama. In May 1996, a prostitute named Mariaty escaped the death penalty but got a life sentence for the manslaughter of another prostitute who was sharing her Geylang room in late-1995. Mariaty, 33, killed her colleague by bashing her head in with a brick, after she'd accused Mariaty of stealing her regular client and tried to claw out Mariaty's eyes with her fingers and break her leg with her feet.

In April 1998, two Malaysian prostitutes were found naked and strangled to death in their Geylang shophouse lodgings near Lorong 24A. The two women — one Malay aged 46, one Chinese aged 32 — had remained undiscovered for nearly two days. The police discovered the decomposing bodies only after reports of a stench stinking out the shophouse. The Malay woman's head was found covered with a towel, with a nylon strip around her neck. An electrical cord was found around Ms Low Toong Lin's neck, and there were blood stains outside the room indicating a struggle.

Inside Geylang's brothels. From the basic bed-and-bathroom combo to well-furnished plush, with mirrors on walls/ceilings, circular beds and sometimes, water beds and sex 'toys'. Not to mention, spicy wall calendars.

Both women were from Kuala Lumpur, and had been robbed of their cash and jewellery.

Male touts and pimps are all around Geylang to supervise the girls and to drum up business from punters. Such men can earn from $3,000–$4,000 a month, though their working hours are long (from 12 noon–4 am). But if the rewards are good, the punishments are stiff if a pimp is caught. In 1993, one such man was jailed for 53 months and fined $21,000, while a housewife got a six-month jail sentence and a $10,000 fine for allowing her Grange Road flat to be used as a contact point for prostitutes.

In February 1995, a 61-year-old part-time cabbie was fined $9,000 for managing a contact point for Thai prostitutes in Tiong Bahru, and for living off their earnings. He was arrested while waiting outside Orchard Parade Hotel for his male client to 'finish' with a Thai girl in his hotel room. The court was told the tout got a $10 cut each time he drove a Thai takeaway to and from her working engagements.

1996 saw big changes to Geylang's streetwalker scene. Regular Anti-Vice action, plus tough immigration procedures at points of entry (such as WTC, from Batam and single Thai girls arriving at Changi), had cut down the numbers of freelancers visibly at work, leaving only a hard-core rump of mainly local women hooking around Lorong 10/12 and Talma Road. While the swish new budget hotels and new apartment blocks opening up along Geylang lorongs (from Lorong 4 through to Lorong 20) severely reduced the old-style lodging houses and little old hotels which freelance girls had used to conduct their business.

What's more, a local property analyst insisted that Geylang itself was becoming a tourist attraction, saying it wasn't just known for its red-light character but was 'also famous for its food specialities'. He added: 'Rather than acting as a deterrent, the red-light character can make the area more colourful.'

At least seven new Geylang budget hotels had opened by end-1996, with the signs of even more to come. Some had opened with an extremely high profile, such as Guillemard Hotel on Lorong 18 — which in February 1996 even hired the very expensive TCS megas, Zoe Tay and Fann Wong, to grace the opening ceremony (at 12.38 pm sharp). This may well have been the sole off-screen occasion upon which the two TV lovelies had visited the very heart of Geylang's viceland!

Just when all these nice new budget hotels were enjoying a good 'rent-by-the-hour' business with hookers and clients or couples seeking privacy (Japanese 'love hotel' style), the Hotel Licencing Board issued a stern edict. In January 1998, all new hotels within Geylang's Designated Red-light Area (DRA) were instructed to cease their short-term transit-rate room hires — or lose their licences. The hotels had been charging around $20 for two hours or $50 for all-day — and some hotels were renting out the same bedroom for as many as eight times per day.

One Geylang hotel executive complained: 'Before this ban, all our 112 rooms were full with many booked by transit guests. Business was so good that there were even people waiting in the lobby for a room to become available.'

The top two TCS-TV drama queens, Zoe Tay and Fann Wong, paid a brief 1996 visit to Geylang for the official opening of Guillemard Hotel.

Spanking new budget hotels keep popping up all around Geylang's naughty bits, radically changing the area's looks.

And it was probably this business dip (fuelled also by plunging regional tourist arrivals in response to South-east Asia's economic crunch) that led three months later in April to a sudden reversal of the short-time ban. The Hotel Licencing Board informed the 50-odd affected hotels that it had reviewed the ruling 'at length' and decided to suspend it — though the HLB did also caution the hotels about renting rooms out to prostitutes.

Geylang hoteliers were naturally relieved, with one on Lorong 10 saying that half of her by-the-hour business had been from local couples — with that 50 percent statistic repeated by a Lorong 12 hotel whose manager added that many of her short-time guests were Filipinas turning up with their boyfriends on Sundays.

ORCHARD ROAD

The key features of Geylang Vice are that its red-light district is well out of town (and thus out of sight?) and that the man must go to the woman who does not and cannot herself solicit. But it's the reverse in Orchard Road's plush hotel-land. And there the pickings are rich: visiting single businessmen, on their own and not short of cash...

The women who patrol the hotel lobby, food outlets, lounges, discos are usually classy dames who don't look — or come — cheap. If they looked cheap, they might be ordered out by hotel security staff or even charged with criminal trespass. But the potential embarrassment factor in accusing a sophisticated looking woman

32

who may actually be a waiting wife or whatever is usually high enough to leave such women alone, as they scan male faces for a 'hit'.

Few hotels refuse access to a woman accompanying a paying male guest, even if somehow she doesn't quite look like his legally wed wife (because she's wearing black fishnet panty hose, microskirt and her boobs are peeping out?!). But some hotels have been known to bump up the room bill to a double from a single if the man has entertained an overnight guest. The drawback with this practice is that it can win such hotels a counterproductive negative reputation with cost-conscious businessmen.

There was a time when hotel-visiting massage services were able to advertise in the Singapore Buying Guide yellow pages phone book, but this was stopped in 1989 if such services could not demonstrate a fixed office address (by and large, they operated through a pager or by phone bookings only — as they were often health centres which were not supposed to arrange 'home visits', nor be quite so explicit about their extra services).

This led to an outbreak of what got called the 'massage card tout menace' in the newspapers. That is, men who either with the collusion of front-desk staff in suggesting likely room numbers or on a mass direct-mail basis would sneak into the hotel and, floor by floor, slip little cards under the bedroom doors.

These cards were to the point. A sample: 'Good massage that will relieve your tiredness. You will never regret my room service. Call for appointment: 3 pm–3 am.' The accompanying illustration was of an alluring young Chinese woman whose blouse buttons appeared to be completely undone. And silly girl, she had absent-mindedly forgotten to put on her bra!

Following the media blitz on these room-service cards, reports of massage girls stealing items from hotel bedrooms and a few tout arrests (they were usually fined about $300 for criminal trespass), the bigger-hotel security guards and closed-circuit camera systems meant that massage cards were now mainly found under the bedroom doors of non-deluxe hotels.

Men on their own in plush hotel rooms and looking for a little action usually know about the health centre (non-gym variety) that is often on the hotel premises (the hotel rents the space to the health centre, it has no control over its operations). For in even the most respectable of hotels, the health centre is usually happy to send a masseuse to the guest's room where she will doubtless offer extras — making the delivery of sexual services to a hotel room almost as straightforward as ordering a room-service cheese sandwich, or a Waldorf Salad in the posher hotels.

ESCORT AGENCIES

But if that approach fails, still restless men could pick up their hotel room Yellow Pages and flick through to its Escort Service section. This comprises 13 pages of entertaining adverts for (mainly Orchard Road area-based) agencies which hire out female (and male) companions. But, for what? And what for?

The phraseology in these adverts is tantalising. 'Charming multiracial ladies and macho guys', 'Dining,

SOCIAL ESCORT SERVICES

We have young attractive, courteous and sophisticated ladies to keep you company for dancing, sightseeing and other social functions to give you a relaxation time after a hectic day. Male Escorts are also available. Call us now and you'll be jubilant and delighted with our discreet services. from Dawn To Dusk. We'll make that difference in your stay here. We accept Credit Cards, Traveller Cheque and Foreign Currencies.

ESCORT SERVICE

FOR A REFRESHING EXPERIENCE OF YOUR LIFE.....
WE HAVE THE PERFECT PEOPLE FOR ALL OCCASIONS AND SOCIAL NEEDS, YOU WILL THANK YOUR LUCKY STARS AND MALE/FEMALE ESCORTS ALSO AVAILABLE
CALL US NOW
DAY & NIGHT

OR VISIT US AT

ALL MAJOR CREDIT CARDS ACCEPTED

(ESCORTS) (DAY & NIGHT)

LET OUR GORGEOUS YOUNG LADIES AND MACHO MEN ATTEND TO YOUR SOCIAL NEEDS... DISCRETION ASSURED. * MODERATE CHARGES

ESCORT SERVICES
Pretty, Courteous, Male & Female Escorts for your social Entertainment
CALL:

Make Your Entertainment Comes Alive With Our Charming Angels of Hearts MALE FEMALE

DANCE AND SHOW AVAILABLE
MAJOR CREDIT CARDS ACCEPTED

Right: With the Yellow Pages, you can let your fingers do the prowling...
Below: The successful legal action taken by local A-list model Hanis against Tiffany escort agency attracted much media attention and proved a Singapore legal landmark.

Defamatory to be linked to escort agency

The court ruled in the recent case involving model Hanis that ads linking reputable persons to such services may affect the public's view of them

IT IS defamatory to link a reputable person to be the business of a social escort agency, as it gives a negative impression about the person to certain sections of the public, the High Court says.

It made the ruling recently when it awarded $30,000 in damages to former top Singapore model Hanis Saini Hussey, who sued a social escort agency for using her picture without her permission in its advertisement in the Yellow Pages' Buying Guide.

In his judgment, Justice Goh Joon Seng considered a 1972 English case in which a well-known London nightclub, Annabel's, restrained an escort agency from using the name "Annabel's Escort Agency".

The English court granted an injunction to the club because the use of its name in the escort agency was a kind of attack on the general goodwill of the club, even though this was unintended.

The club, the court held, was entitled to hold this view: "If it is going to be thought by a sufficient number of people that we are somehow associated with the running of an escort agency."

THE LAW PAGE
By TAN OOI BOON

some of the tar will come off on us."

Justice Goh said there amount to be a similar connotation surrounding social escort agencies here.

He noted that this was confirmed by the owner of Tiffany Promotions, the escort agency sued by Miss Hussey.

When asked whether it was true that escort agencies provided sexual services for a lie, the owner of Tiffany replied: "It's a gossip. I cannot control people's tongues."

In Miss Hussey's case, the

court noted that the 30-year-old mother of three had gained considerable fame, as she was the first Singapore model to have achieved international success.

In her 12-year career, she had appeared in top fashion magazines such as Vogue, Bazaar and Marie Claire.

In Singapore, she also appeared in various publications including The Straits Times, Her World and Go.

In 1992, she helped Action for Aids to promote Aids awareness and the use of condoms by modelling for a picture, in which she wore a

tight-fitting black cheongsam.

In 1996, she came upon the escort agency's Yellow Pages advertisement, featuring that picture of her in the cheongsam.

She started receiving phone calls from her friends teasing her about her "new line of work".

Her parents also called her and demanded to know how she was involved with the agency.

The defence's case was that the picture in its advertisement was not that of Miss Hussey.

It said that the picture was that of "a Chinese girl", one that was drawn by a roadside artist from China who operated during the Chinese New Year.

But Justice Goh said: "A comparison of the picture with

the picture in the advertisement would totally discredit the defendant."

He added that in view of Miss Hussey's high-profile modelling career and the wide circulation of the Aids campaign print, a sizeable section of the public would link the escort agency's advertisement to her.

So, the advertisement was defamatory of the ex-model, it ruled.

The court also considered the conduct of the defence in suggesting, without evidence, that Miss Hussey was herself a part-time social escort with an agency called High Society Escort & Hostess Services.

The defendant has appealed to the Court of Appeal.

Court refers to Chiam's case

IN ASSESSING the damages for Miss Hanis Saini Hussey, the High Court studied another defamation suit, one which involved opposition MP Chiam See Tong.

In the 1986 case, the MP for Potong Pasir had sued the Kin Zhang Piang restaurant for using his photograph in an advertisement without his permission.

The picture was taken when he was attending a birthday dinner at the restaurant with his party supporters. A fund-raising karaoke session was held at the dinner, in which those present were asked to sing. Mr Chiam was invited to sing, and he raised $1,000.

A few weeks later, the restaurant used a photograph of him holding a microphone in an advertisement to promote its menu. Next to it were two captions, in Chinese and in English.

The Chinese version read: "Member of Parliament Chiam See Tong's simple song Hong Hio Xin raised $1,000." The English one, which did not refer to him, stated: "Charity Fund collection/Community Chest actively dedication songs are welcome."

The court awarded

$50,000 in damages to Mr Chiam. It found that the advertisement suggested that the MP had consented to the use of his photograph for publicity, either for gain or to sponsor a private restaurant.

The court said that a substantial number of people who saw that advertisement would have thought less of him as it would seem that he had taken advantage of his position.

The social escort agency's advertisement (right) is a lookalike of the photo (left) posed by Hanis for an Aids awareness campaign.

dancing, etc', 'Why hesitate? (discreet service)', 'We have pretty and charming young girls to serve you', 'Make your stay enjoyable with our sweet and lovely escorts', 'Lonely? You can be close to someone right here by dialling (day or night)...', 'For pretty and energetic ladies, call...' — and so on.

Of course, all those adverts with their drawings of their alluring escorts may well be simply offering agreeable and attractive companions for the dinner table or the disco. Or even to share a man's excitement as he thrills to the spectacle of Sentosa's Musical Fountain in action. You never know.

In April 1998, top local model Hanis won her defamation suit against an escort agency which had used her alleged likeness in a Yellow Pages advert for its 'charming and elegant ladies' services. Hanis said in court: 'The last thing I wanted was to be associated with a social escort agency... (which is) basically high-class prostitution.' For its part, the agency owner denied that social escort work had any sexual connotations.

Male escorts are most often booked by visiting Caucasian businessmen, rather than frisky local *tai-tais* or other 'dabbling' women, who tend to simply want a handsome dining companion and capable dance partner for the evening, rather than actual sex. Caucasian men, meanwhile, can make most strange requests of their virile young male escorts.

One newspaper report told the tale of how one such young man was asked to cut his client's underpants. While they were still on him. The escort had to snip carefully, while his client's excitement mounted. And, displaying a truly *kiasu* attitude, the escort was quoted as complaining: 'If he wanted to get rid of his underwear, why didn't he give them to me? After all, they were very expensive, about $80 each.' The male escort had missed the point of this admittedly peculiar ritual!

ORCHARD TOWERS

By daytime, this is an orthodox mid-range Orchard Road shopping centre. But once darkness falls, Orchard Towers starts jumping, the girls start arriving — and the complex shows why it is cheekily and cheerily known as 'four floors of whores'. For here the women are locals, Thais, Malaysians, Indonesians; all sorts and most price categories. The budget section lurks around the steps leading into the centre from Orchard Road, or just inside the lobby. These women try to hook their catch before the man gets inside and is thus able to appreciate the wide choice range of available females in its pubs, clubs and discos.

In early-1997 however, a stern notice appeared outside erstwhile hotspot Club 392. This warned: 'No soliciting or immoral activities allowed in the club.' Inside, the club was looking under-populated and under-energised, even with the (still not-so-good) live music pumping out. It marked a complete U-turn in Club 392 policy.

For this ground-level joint had previously been wall-to-wall girls pressing for tender bids from the many men there precisely because they knew they wouldn't have to gift these women with flowers or chocolate boxes to win their (temporary) favours. Why, the joint would get so crowded that a man's choice of female partner was determined by whom he found himself crushed up (closely) against. As for the girls, up till around 11 pm they tried to fit in 'short-times' before returning to the bar where they'd then aim to get hired on an overnight basis. Inside Club 392, there were very few virgins.

But with the club's 1997 policy-reversal, Thai working girls lost a useful basecamp. Their response was to spread out elsewhere, such as into Orchard Towers' basement (though this was favoured by Filipinas), old favourites upstairs in the complex or to well-known singles bars on Scotts Road.

Still thriving was Ginivy's country-and-western bar to the rear of Orchard Towers (over Jason's supermarket), a joint preferred by Indonesian girls — though there were also Thais and local ladies (plus a tiny band of 'exotics' from Laos). Ginivy's offered a lot of visual entertainment as women of pleasure dived in-and-out to check out its male customer potential. For this joint is a friendly sort of place, with a fairly regular clientele enjoying the live 'Singapore cowboy' music and its female allure. But women on their own in here would much rather men didn't say 'Looking only'.

Also in Orchard Towers are more upmarket — and more orthodox — niteries. The classier, pricier hookers enjoy these joints: the atmosphere, the music and the (Caucasian, black American and Middle East) male pickings. Though most women in these two venues are locals on a night out, good-time party-girls or disco-bunnies — who may or may not be looking for male company. But either way, it's always the man who's buying at least the drinks.

THAI TAKEAWAYS

Thai girls, whose looks or ages deny them access to the town's fleshpots, stick to servicing Thai building workers — either using the Golden Mile 'Little Thailand' shopping centre on Beach Road as their base camp or going in organised groups by van on weekends to those building sites where Thai workers live in makeshift wooden huts.

One Thai prostitute who plied her trade around Singapore's worksites turned up in the papers in February 1996 when a policeman was jailed for a week and fined $1,000 after having sex with her in his car. The 21-year-old policeman (and his 20-year-old colleague, both of whom were off-duty and in plainclothes at the time) stopped the woman while she was out walking with a male friend near Kranji. When she could not produce valid documents, she was 'invited' through crude hand gestures into the car and driven to Neo Tiew Road, near Lim Chu Kang.

There and then, the policeman had sex with her in the back seat, after which she gave his colleague a quick hand-job. This ill-assorted group were spotted by an orthodox police patrol, and charges of conduct prejudicial to the good order and discipline of the Singapore Police Force by having sex with a prostitute in a car parked on a public road were levelled against the policeman. He was also charged for failing to take action against a person whom he had reasonable grounds to suspect was an illegal immigrant. A rape charge

Thai girls await Thai business near Golden Mile's 'Little Thailand' shopping centre along Beach Road.

against him was dropped.

It emerged at his trial that the Thai takeaway had arrived in Singapore in October 1995 using another woman's passport and had plied her trade almost exclusively around local worksites.

In March 1998, a Sunday night swoop on a large Kranji lodging house found a sex party in full swing for foreign construction workers. Eight hookers (mainly Thai, one a China national) were handed over to police after the private security firm's raid. Two of the women were in action, dancing naked under a dim light, when the raiders suddenly broke in. It emerged that the women had charged $20 for 20-minute solo sex sessions with the foreign workers, with each woman having sex with seven to eight men per night. All eight woman had condoms with them and between them, they had over $1,000 in cash from their 'full monty' nightwork around the lodging house circuit.

INDONESIANS

The well-defined streetwalker sector for Indonesian women in Geylang lies between Lorongs 10/12, and along Talma Road. Too well-defined sometimes, as police car patrols are frequent here — and the small boarding houses used by Indonesian women for bonking can get raided by Anti-Vice police.

One result is that the girls step outside only at certain times: usually during the 6–8 pm early evening period (looking for short-times) and then after 11 pm (looking for all-nights) when, according to one boarding house owner, 'even Anti-Vice wants to relax'. Such promenades are well-known to the many foreign workers who board up in this area and who regard the women as an entertaining free gawk-show at nights.

This exasperates the women as there's rarely business on offer from such oglers and their huddles can attract unwanted police attention. Here, I overheard one woman try to explain to an Indian worker her terms. He hadn't understood exactly what she meant by an hourly rate, so she spelt it out: 'One hour means one time — you quick, hour quick, OK?'

A bigger problem than Anti-Vice for these female visitors from Batam comes at Immigration desks at WTC, where Batam/Bintan ferries arrive. There, officials may make inspired guesses at the women's real 'reasons for visit', and give them a three-days-only social visit pass. This cuts down on their money-making chances, so hard-working Indonesian women are very happy indeed if they can return to Batam, exhausted but richer by $1,000. Their usual earnings come in much lower than this, but the strength of the Singapore dollar compared to Indonesia's rupiah compensates.

Sometimes, Immigration officials won't let 'known' women in at all — demanding that they show sufficient cash for their alleged shopping trips or sending them straight back again and making it plain they cannot re-attempt entry to Singapore for at least one month.

But Indonesia's economic meltdown and post-Suharto turbulence provoked newspaper reports that 'tens of thousands of women' were turning to prostitution to support their families, with a *Jakarta Post* headline in August 1998 screaming 'Crisis prompts prostitution explosion'. A Yogyakarta-based charity estimated that Indonesia now had at least 650,000 women selling sex in some form, while some sociologists put this figure even higher. WTC Immigration officials are doubtless aware of these troubling figures.

INDIANS

Indian women (that is, women specially 'imported' from India — usually from Tamil Nadu) naturally look to Serangoon Road for conducting their business. Especially on Sunday afternoons, such women clad in alluring, colourful saris or Punjabi suits patrol a strip of Little India, using always-busy Serangoon Plaza as their focal point.

Either their pimp or they themselves approach likely looking male passers-by, and spell out the offer and the charges. These range from $50–$60 for short-times, $120–$150 for overnights — depending on age and looks. These rates can drop as night falls, with $100 being accepted for overnights. Their target market is visiting Indian tourists or Indian workers on their day off, and they do most of their 'work' in the side-street lodging houses or small hotels in this area.

With increased police surveillance of their activities, these Indian women can try tricks like wearing neck-chains that look like a traditional Indian married woman's ornamentation and pretend they are merely waiting for their husbands. In 1992, 42 such Indian women (in their early-20s to mid-30s) were deported for having overstayed their social visit visas; their operators (Singaporean, Malaysian but mainly Indian) were heavily fined.

There's behind-closed-doors action down the side-streets off Serangoon Road. In 1993, a 'Touch Me Naked' girlie bar on Syed Alwi Road was exposed by a newspaper, which reported that inside this dark bar with its high-backed seat-cubicles were 20 girls in their 20s (mainly Malaysian), of whom eight would disrobe for male customers who paid them a $20 fee. This allowed the men a 10-minute private peep show by shining a (supplied) torch or their lighters on interesting parts of the girls' thus-revealed anatomies.

Some girls reportedly allowed: 'Can See — and Can Touch.' If sex-for-sale was later agreed, it would take place off the premises and would cost $100 a short-time. The bar sold its beer for the very high price of $22 per bottle, and also reportedly had a back-of-the-house VIP room for big private parties.

FILIPINAS

Filipinas have also left a mark on Singapore's sex-for-sale industry. Out-and-out Pinay hooking here is rare, with occasional reports of girls lured here from Manila on a 'holiday now, pay later' basis. Such Filipinas often find themselves installed in a mildly infamous old apartment estate just off River Valley Road. From here, they sally forth to prearranged clients at hotels where they perform short-time sex for the (comparatively high) rates of $100–$150. The short-time rates at the apartment block itself apparently went on a $50–$100 scale.

Chinatown's People's Park food centre (above) where Filipina working girls (below) used to hang out in large numbers.

In 1996, a Chinese man and Filipina woman were convicted for running a prostitution racket out of this River Valley Rd apartment block. When Anti-Vice police raided the flat, they found five Filipinas in residence on a sex-for-sale basis. The man, a 49-year-old, got a 9-month sentence and a $50,000 fine, having faced eight charges (five for pimping, three for importing prostitutes into Singapore). The woman, a 26-year-old, faced five pimping charges and was fined $24,000.

It emerged from their court case that the Filipina 'imports' hunted male clients in Peyton Place, an entertainment joint in the Orchard Towers basement. The prostitutes had charged $200 for overnight sex, and $80 for short-times. They were obliged to hand over all their earnings to the pimping couple till they had repaid the cost of bringing them to Singapore (each Filipina had paid $3,600 for airfares, documents, etc).

It is also a dark fear of Singaporean employers that their maids may be engaging in 'ECA' at home on weekdays. There was that notable Hougang case in 1993 when an employer grew suspicious after her three-year-old son lay down on her body, lifted her skirt — and shouted: '$20!' What's more, food had been disappearing suspiciously speedily in this household, the telephone line was too often engaged during the day, and the maid was buying clothes and jewellery she could hardly have afforded on her modest maid's wages.

But this was very much a rare case. Only a tiny number of employed Filipina maids do this sort of thing despite the financial temptations. Indeed, when a newspaper ran a 1992 story over-dramatically headlined 'Psst! Know what your maid's up to?', a group of maids wrote thus in response to the paper:

'We are truly aghast. The article is demoralising. We are just maids... Do you know the result of the article? Well, if not, we will tell you. Some maids are no longer allowed to go out every Sunday for fellowship... Their day-off has now been changed to once a month, and this day is used to go out and shop for their personal needs... Do bear in mind that we are here to work as domestic helpers, not anything else...'

HOSTESS LOUNGES

Singapore's many hostess lounges range from the extremely glitzy and plush members' clubs to the small, dark and smoky brandy bars. One of the differences between the two ends of this niche market is that girls working in the plush clubs would rather be called 'guest relations officers', while those women in its lower reaches are doomed to be tagged 'bargirls'.

Taking their style from over-the-top Hongkong nightclubs (such as the famous Club Volvo before the Swedish car-maker had its legal way and got its name changed to Bboss), the members' clubs can cost millions to kit out. Their opulent interiors comprise deep carpets, black marble, luxurious sofas, pricey art works, the full works — all designed to spell 'you're wealthy, so spend'.

These clubs can take up whole floors in shopping centres. They are popular mainly with English-speaking executives, professionals and Japanese men who splash out on expensive brandy. If their companies do

The monthly income advertised in this advert is $4,000 to $6,000 per month. But that high figure includes tips, commissions — and maybe more to come?

not sponsor corporate memberships, individual members must pay at least $1,000 to join — with annual fees of $500 and up.

The very pretty hostesses who work in these members' clubs are usually under 25, speak English and are educated to at least Secondary Two level. Some have A levels, and a few also speak Japanese. And during school holidays or after exams, cute schoolgirls — in pursuit of cash for those oh-so-essential brand name clothes — reportedly do stints as hostesses (and even as social escorts). All hostesses are expected to wear dinner gowns slashed to the thigh-top and high heels; sometimes they undergo training programmes to brush up on dressing, conversation skills, etiquette, dancing and attitude.

Attitude does matter. A 19-year-old hostess at such a members' club was quoted as saying: 'A good hostess is someone who is able to entertain her guest and make him come back to request for her. How much a guest likes a girl depends on how well she presents herself, her behaviour, her ability to socialise and how well she carries out her table service — offering a hot towel, mixing his drink, making sure his glass is always dry, lighting his cigarette, changing ashtrays the moment there are two cigarette butts in it.'

Yes, it's basically an old-style pre-feminist era pampering for which male customers are charged at least $40 per hour. They are also expected to give generous tips if happy with the girl, and further commissions come her way if she uncorks an expensive bottle for her male guest. Anything else and extras are up to the parties involved. Some hostesses do, some don't.

NIGHTCLUBS

The curtain that concealed what really happened in Chinese nightclubs was ripped open in October 1994, after the near-fatal shooting at a Katong shopping centre of mama-san Mona Koh. Suddenly the newspapers were full of such details as how much a mama-san can earn (up to $50,000 a month), how much money gets spent in such nightclubs by male customers ($10,000–$15,000 a night, and mostly on company expenses?) — and how alluring the scent of such big bucks is to the young, pretty and extremely sexy hostesses who work there (200–300 of them per major club).

These girls can earn up to $300 per an eight-hour night from tips alone. That is, if they pleased their clients and let the men grope them a bit and all that. Of course, if the hostesses did decide to provide 'extra-curricular' sex, they could earn heaps more (from $500 up to, reportedly, even $5,000).

As one Chinese businessman told *The Straits Times*: 'Entertaining in nightclubs is part of the business culture here. I supply products to companies in Taiwan, China and Hongkong. When owners of these companies are in town, they want to have drinks in nightclubs and then take pretty girls back to their hotels. In business, you have to play the game. If not, they will go to competitors.'

Wives of such businessmen can take a different view, with one quoted as saying: 'No matter how much you trust your husband, when you put men, liquor and pretty girls together, anything can happen.'

One nightclub mama-san said of the hostesses who earned her such a handsome living: 'I don't force the girls to have sex. They themselves say yes to the man. They are not prostitutes. They only sleep if they like the man. Prostitutes sleep with everybody.' She added that she does try to insist that such men 'put on the raincoat' (ie, use condoms) for their sex with her girls: 'But I'm not sure if they all use.'

Swish Chinese nightclubs also provide entertainment in the form of singers and dancers, with occasional guest appearances by fluffy Taiwanese songbirds or Hongkong movie Category 3 (adult explicit sex) actresses.

Down a small step are the cabarets (sometimes with live stage acts by performers from Hongkong and Taiwan), nightclubs and fancy karaoke lounges that are preferred by Chinese-speaking *towkay* businessmen. The karaoke joints have been growing in popularity at the expense of the cabarets/nightclubs, especially those that have invested millions in their fancy private rooms and KTV facilities. Karaoke hostesses sit and sing with their guests, and encourage them to buy costly drinks.

Sometimes, karaoke hostesses are too obliging and too bold — and police on their routine checks catch them out. In March 1995, the licensee of a Middle Road lounge was fined $3,000 for allowing two teenaged hostesses to go topless in a private KTV room. One undraped-boobs girl was dancing, the other was sitting on a client's lap.

Many karaoke lounges do indeed seem to offer men more than the chance to ruin good songs, with those hostesses who sit with their clients, inflate their drinks bill, flatter their voices… and then? A 1996 *Her World* magazine article inflamed the suspicions of housewives whose husbands spent rather a lot of time at 'business meetings' in karaoke lounges. And rather a lot of money, too.

In the HW article, one aggrieved wife insisted her errant middle-aged husband had spent over $40,000 in five months on a 21-year-old karaoke hostess, including buying her a $6,000 Cartier watch, membership of a fancy women's fitness club, brandname shopping sprees, weekends together in Kuala Lumpur — and offers to buy her a semi-D in her Malaysian hometown of Ipoh and even a $2.2m Orchard Rd apartment as a love nest. When the wife answered a property agent's call at her home about this proposed district 9 flat, even she could tell something was amiss.

So, she set about investigating her husband's karaoke activities with the help of a private dick — and soon she had incriminating photos, credit card receipts and the like, all of which told the true story of those business meetings. The wife noted how such hostesses compared their male clients by the cars they drove, watches they wore, what they would spend on a hostess per night — and the potential 'big sweep' of setting a hostess up in her own flat.

Eventually, this dogged wife confronted the hostess (by phone), and discovered her husband had slept with her only once — in a hotel, for which he'd paid $500. She heard her cynical rival say this: 'It is very difficult to find a one-woman man. Especially if he is a businessman. They have a lot of money to spend.'

So the still-sore housewife warned other (presumably now well-worried) *Her World* readers: 'Beware the male company your husband keeps — he can pick up bad habits from womanising pals'!

Next on the ladder comes what's called Japanese lounges, followed by straightforward hostess lounges. At both, the girls are again young, pretty, glamorous and sexy; and again, extras are often arranged. The main role of such hostesses is to act understanding, cute and sexy — to ensure the booze flows freely.

The accumulated income between salary, commissions and tips is enough for most girls (between $2,000 and $3,000). Other financially ambitious hostesses regard this as just the basic income, and strive to double their earnings through extra services. For part-time hostesses, it's payment by the hour — on average $30 (usually higher for weekend nights), again with extras up to them.

These part-timers can include undergraduates financing their way through higher education and/or making extras for those little fripperies. One such, an attractive 20-year-old, described her night job to *The New Paper*: 'All I have to do is drink and smoke with the customers. Of course, they touch me and all that, but it's no big deal. The best thing is I get paid for it. Each night I earn at least $150. It's like getting paid for partying.'

The down-market music lounges are concentrated in old shophouses around Serangoon/Balestier Roads, Geylang, Katong and Joo Chiat. They often have highly entertaining names, and all give nothing away with their outside visuals — closed-in and blank, with the small door as the only opening. Inside, it's not much clearer because these joints are so dark. So deliberately dark. Male drinkers sometimes cannot see their own hands, nor those of his bargirl companion. Though he can sure feel what she's sometimes doing with them…

Such bars are mostly very Chinese. When I bravely went into one, my hostess put pumpkin seeds into my mouth any time I opened it. This solved the no-conversation problem. Through my male companion, I asked for a different hostess. I was asked whether I wanted 'big or small'. I sought further clarification. It emerged that the size specification referred to breasts. I replied I wasn't too fussed, so long as some English was possible. My new (small) companion declared an early interest in my own dimensions. Talking in terms of inches, she was most anxious to compare the length in question with those of the Chinese men to whom she was more accustomed. She even threatened to fetch a tape measure. I left her a $10 tip, and left. The sunshine outside was almost blinding after the near-total darkness inside the music lounge…

MASSAGE SALONS

In May 1998, a married couple were found guilty on charges relating to the use of Balmoral Park Inn Health Centre in Balmoral Plaza basement as a brothel. They were each fined $3,000 and the massage salon's licence was revoked. During a vivid 8-day trial, the court heard how police raids on the salon had found two masseuses having sex with their clients and another masseuse dressed merely in her bra and panties. A large number of condoms had also been found on the premises.

One masseuse told the court she'd engaged in 'ex-

Typical massage adverts, with a new trend — men massaging. Bottom right: Inside an actual massage room, just the bare essentials.

tra services' on a daily basis, charging $50 for masturbation and $100–150 for full sex. These 'extras', testified the 23-year-old, were a private matter between her and her client, adding that she got an $11 cut from the salon's hourly rate of $50 for basic massage. She agreed that she'd had sex with paying customers in all other massage salons she'd worked in before. And she added that she kept her condoms in a Milo tin (another masseuse said she kept her condoms in a teapot) as her boss had told her it was 'very dangerous' to keep condoms in her lockers.

From outside, Singapore's 80 over health/sauna/massage centres (in hotel complexes and shopping centres, mainly) look perfectly legitimate. And inside, too. But it's the health centres that do only proper, no 'hanky-panky' massages (such as that attached to the Singapore Badminton Association) that are better known. The newspaper display adverts for health centres suggest the true story.

For a start, on the basis of these ads, no woman would think of going into a health centre for a massage — unless she was decidedly naive. The adverts show pretty girls (described as charming, gentle, young, attentive, etc) going about their massage techniques on men's backs — though the girls in these advert photos are, it seems, rarely the actual girls who do the massaging. Technically, there are strict rules governing what can (or, more importantly, cannot) take place within health centres — but regular male patrons will know all about, and expect, the extra services that are on offer at an extra price.

Sometimes, with fatal results. In September 1993,

an elderly man (said to be about 60 years of age) was found dead in a hotel health centre massage room. One offered reason for his sudden death was a heart attack, brought on after the masseuse had stood and walked on his back (not a form of physical assault, but a standard massage practice!). A health centre spokeswoman said: 'He knew most of the girls here and was quite friendly with them.'

The masseuses can even be undergraduate part-timers. One such, a 21-year-old, was saving up to do an overseas Master's degree by working at a Orchard Road posh hotel's health centre, where she performed sexual services that stopped short of actual intercourse. She shocked newspaper readers by explaining: 'I don't just do the "special services" for any client who asks for them, I only do them for those who are decent and reasonably young.'

She did 10 am to 5 pm daytime-only shifts, thus avoiding the post-work 'rush hour' and the late-night stuff. Even so, she earned at least $200 a day. This was made up of the $10 cut for each customer she massaged (on average, four per day), plus all the extras she made for 'special services' (ranging from $50–$150, depending on exactly how special the special services were). Meaning, whether she did hand relief with her top and/or her bra off, whether she allowed him to fondle her boobs, and so on (but again, no sexual intercourse).

DESKER ROAD

Far more direct in its approach is Desker Road, the strip that's become virtually synonymous with Singapore's sex-for-sale trade. It's been that way for many decades, and broad-minded Caucasian visitors to Singapore who want to see what they imagine the 'colourful' old Far East looked like, should not be disappointed by Desker Road.

The vice actually happens in the back-alley between Desker and Rowell Roads, running nearly all the way from Serangoon Road through to Jalan Besar. It is thus unlikely that unknowing people could accidentally find their way into this alley, neatly hidden as it is from the scrutiny of regular Serangoon Road passers-by.

The Desker Road women sit in their little cane chairs and wait inside the back-porches; by and large, they do not solicit unless a man steps inside, when it is thus assumed he has taken the initiative. But the men are mainly 'browsing only', for Desker Road is by day and by night like an anthill of men-in-motion. They walk up and down, side to side, looking and looking and the women can quickly tell whether a man is serious or just window-shopping (when they'll ignore him or if that doesn't work, swear — or even spit — at him).

Also along the alleyway are little shops, virility oil and pill peddlers, cure-all lotion sellers, *fantan* or *Sik-Po* style gambling games (with much money changing hands) or the simple Find-The-Lady three-card tricks at $10 a guess, tiny stalls with extraordinary arrays of sexy video tapes, photos, condoms and sex aids (such as little furry 'penis rings' that look more like what fly-fishermen use), and the alley's famous auspicious temple pythons, bored and curled up in their strong red-painted iron cages 'guarding' the money superstitious men donate.

Desker Road, Singapore's 'backbone of vice' alleyway, reaches from Serangoon Road to near Jalan Besar.

For sale in Desker Road: unusual sex devices.

The alleyway's famous temple pythons can baffle the tourists.

Desker Road is not a pretty sight. Frankly, it's crumbling, dank and smelly. There again, it never was pretty — not even in 1954. That was when a leading local newspaper writer of those times, Sit Yin Fong, produced a vivid column headlined: 'I Am Ashamed Of This.' In his purple-prose piece, he wrote: 'Desker Road is a picture of human tragedy. In an ill-lit, stinking back lane, clusters of Chinese women stand at the open back doors of a long row of shophouses. They are there for "inspection", as one might inspect cattle at a sale.

'Men stop to peer within breathing distance at a woman. They look her up and down, and down and up, turn her round this way and that way, and make lewd remarks...

'Vice is cheap here — the cheapest in the city. A woman can be had for the price of three beers...

'I once took a walk through Desker back lane and met more embarrassed familiar faces than I cared to count. The women are the derelicts who once knew a better existence, and there is no worse end...'

Another down-to-earth account of Desker activity came in a 1991 local novel with the vivacious title *Lusts From The Underworld*. Describing basement-rate sex (this one for $12, below even the basic $30), the author wrote: 'There on the bed lay an overweight woman. Her dentures were on a table next to the bed. Her skirt was lifted up. Between her huge thighs was a slender naked male body, his bottom half pumping rhythmically. Both the faces could not be seen — his above her body, and hers hidden by the evening newspaper she was reading.'

What's more, the woman was chiding the bobbing

Above: Desker Road alley-
ways have rooms like this.
An average of four women
are inside each 'waiting
room'.
Right: In Serangoon Road,
looking out for Indian business.

man thus (in Hokkien) for being too slow: 'Hurry up, little fellow! How big is your $12?' Charming, no? And perfectly possible off Desker Road.

FLANDERS SQUARE

Further up (and off) Serangoon Road, there's another red-light zone which is less tacky than, indeed a few notches up from, Desker Road — even if in Hokkien it's known as 'Banana Backyard'. It's off Petain Road, bounded by the backsides of Marne Road and Flanders Square, and again would only be noticed by those who were actually looking for it. On one side, it's terraced houses, the other a row of apartments. But inside, the arrangement is much the same in both — corridor-style rows going through the buildings at ground-floor level, with little individual cubicles leading off both sides (plus some similar rooms upstairs).

Unlike the system off Desker Road (where the women gather in the porch and share the cubicles), each Flanders Square girl has her own little room for which she pays a rent (and often, some 'protection' money). She will either sprawl on her little bed or stand guard on her doorstep if looking for business or wanting a chat with a neighbour. A minority of the rooms work rather like taxi shifts, in that two girls may use the same room as their 'office' during any one Flanders Square daily session (its hours are roughly 1–10 pm).

This own-room system means the little cubicles can look like personalised teenage girls' small bedrooms with washing facilities attached, or even like a girls'

WELCOME UPSTAIR
1ST FLOOR
WE HAVE PRETTY GIRLS
FOR MASSAGE AND OTHERS
SERVICE

欢迎光临
请上二楼
楼摩服按週到
谢々

WELCOME TO UPSTAIR
WE HAVE MASSAGE
AND OTHER SERVICE

全能服务

按摩句

FLANDERS SQUARE

In Flanders Square, the writing is on the wall! Centre: Entrance to Flanders Square. Bottom: A clear view from New Park Hotel?

college hall of residence (though the Flanders Square ideas on Home Economics might be different from those of most other girls). Some have pin-up pictures (Aaron Kwok, Jackie Chan, Chow Yun Fatt, etc), some have soft cushions and toys, some have sound systems or even small TV sets — while inside and out (as in Desker Road) there are colourful Use Condoms posters in the four national languages. And a few rooms have their own blunt messages, with signs like: 'No condoms, I don't work!' alongside the usual 'No spitting' and 'No waiting' orders.

It's a small but dense red-light strip (about 20 houses with corridors, with from 10–16 cubicles off each of them), overlooked by the Kitchener Road front side of New Park Hotel. But high-up hotel guests will not see 'hot action' from their bedroom windows: the Flanders Square girls, unless they're taking a break, stay strictly indoors. Their corridors are half-lit by appropriately red or pink neon lights, while a locked cubicle door will mean its occupant is on her break or away — or, if her light box is switched on, is busy inside. At least two locked doors had 'gone away' signs stuck to them, giving the date of the girls' anticipated return to the 'office'.

So men walk through and out the other side, and along the next-door corridor and so on, again usually just browsing but sometimes hunting out a suitable short-time partner. In typically banal 'how-much?' fashion, this can mean haggling for the girl who will go for the cheapest price — no matter what her looks, age, etc. Some girls can get a certain reputation: I was told of one who 'lets you do it standing up, and for just $30!'

Curious, I checked out her room number. Her door was locked, with her light on — she was busy inside. But right outside her door were three more men, either waiting for their turn or waiting for their pal to finish inside.

The men who swarm through the corridors of Flanders Square are of all races, and all ages — including some youngsters who could well be schoolboys on an exciting don't-tell-Mummy look-look outing. And including many (married?) men who would much rather not meet other people of their prior acquaintance in places like this. I've met three men who were decidedly embarrassed to hear my cheery call of 'How's tricks?' when we encountered each other in these back lanes: one explained his pursuit of this version of sex thus: 'It eliminates the need for courtship.'

Without actually soliciting (they're technically not allowed to), the Flanders Square girls will indicate their interest and availability to men stopping by their doors with some plain-speaking words — and they will reject men whose looks, manners or whatever do not appeal. Very few of the girls speak any English, most of them are Chinese. A good many of them look seriously sexy, as they lean seductively against their doors or recline wantonly on their beds, wearing clothes which make it plain they're not librarians or accountants — and which attract male eyes to their most alluring body parts.

Here, they charge a little more than do their 'cousins' off Desker Road. There are two basic Flanders Square standard operating procedures: one is that s*ck and f*ck combo (with condom on all the time) for an average $50. The seasoned girls will aim to have all this finished within ten minutes. Two, for between $60 and $80 and taking about 15 minutes, initially involves a 'body massage'. This means the now topless girl sprinkling her breasts with baby powder and leaning over the man who is lying on his back, then brushing his chest with her talc-coated breasts. This leads on to the sex itself.

Other girls offer a body massage alone, charging $20 for 10 minutes' worth (or till the man has reached a climax — whichever comes first). Other girls (the least good-looking ones) offer an ordinary *bedek-bedek* (pretend) massage for $15 or even $13, with 'hand-jobs' at extra cost.

Outside, as with Desker Road, there's that 'Far East seaport bazaar' mix of gambling, snake-oil peddlers and fortune-tellers, and a busy day-and-night bustling men-only crowd.

Just some 50m away from Flanders Square is one of Singapore's most splendid shophouse rows. Fully restored by mid-1998, the 18 shophouses along Petain Road were then inspected by *The Straits Times* which noted: 'It sits in an area that was known for its red-light activities'. 'Was'? Why, just down the road, Flanders Square is still very much in red-light action — adding its alleged 'historical colour' to the Petain Road shophouses!

A Flanders Square footnote. Until 1987, Singapore Netball Association members had to use the bordering netball court on Petain Road for their training sessions and actual matches. As SNA president Mrs Ivy Singh-Lim put it: 'It was an absolute embarrassment just to be seen there. We even had to tell the foreign teams to ignore taxi-drivers who might insist it was the wrong place.' It's not hard to picture the raucous men that would briefly desert Flanders' honeypots to ogle decent netballing women in their floppy skirts!

KEONG SAIK ROAD

The system is only slightly different at Chinatown's red-light strip along the midway stretch of Keong Saik Road, the weather-worn remnant of the infamous old Kreta Ayer 'Blue Triangle' of vice. These are four-storey walk-ups and the road number lightboxes outside the front doors tell whether their bedrooms are 'womanned' or not. Keong Saik Road basically caters for Chinese men only and there is little visible evidence of its female workforce on the street itself, unless the girls are checking out for a meal break or whatever.

If there's not much going on outside, there can be high drama inside Chinatown's brothels. In January 1996, a prostitute was sentenced to death for murdering a younger and 'more popular' colleague at a Teck Lim Road brothel in August 1995.

Convicted was 36-year-old Teo Kim Hong, who had stabbed 26-year-old Ching Bee Ing (from Sarawak and nicknamed Toto) seven times with a diver's knife. Brothel owner (68-year-old Soong Yoke Chun) had testified that Toto was the 'most popular' of her four employees, and had charged $100 for short-time sex — while Teo's standard rate of $35 was the brothel's 'lowest'. Teo was said to have been angry with Toto because she'd had sex with her (Teo's) boyfriend — and had told

Keong Saik Road: Chinese girls cater for Chinese men in what remains of China-town's old 'Blue Triangle'.

others that Teo offered a special service of oral sex for $30. Teo Kim Hong was hanged in Changi Prison in August 1996.

1995 saw a turning point for Keong Saik Road, as many of its old shophouses became restored yuppie haunts. Especially with the swish $20 million Royal Peacock boutique hotel which spread along a row of 10 shophouses. The Peacock made the most of this dramatic change of use, saying in its publicity that the road was 'once notorious for its red lanterns and ladies of the night'. The hotel added that 'the name Keong Saik Road still manages to raise the odd eyebrow today'. As Michael Jowett, the hotel operator's principal, put it: 'Every taxi driver knows where Keong Saik Road is!'

By 1997, the transformation of the old Blue Triangle was extraordinary, with gentrification almost complete. Of the 85 or so still-standing shophouses here, 28 had been turned into small hotels (most of which insisted they did not do short-time rates) while restaurants, bars and trendy offices had taken over many others. Only 18 walk-in brothels could be counted, and even many of these had been stylishly renovated, at least on the outside.

Keong Saik Road burst into the news in December 1996, when police rejected liquor licences for a couple of dinky new bar/cafes — insisting that the street was 'a relatively quiet residential area'. This made many smirk in bemusement, as they pondered on the 'residential' activities for which Keong Saik Road had been so famous for over 100 years.

TEENAGE SEX

Of all the shock disclosures from the world of Singaporean sex-for-sale in recent times, none provoked such public reaction as when it was reported that teenage girls were offering themselves for money — to buy the clothes, shoes and other brand-named status symbols modern Singaporeans value so highly but which most teenagers could not otherwise afford.

It was the January 1992 issue of *GO* magazine that broke the story. It interviewed a half-dozen teenagers (all anonymously, with the youngest two aged 15, and one a 17-year-old boy) who had done sex in exchange for money. Why? *GO* explained: 'These girls are doing it on the side to fulfil emotional needs, and for frills like nice clothes and shoes and other treats for themselves. It is all the more incongruous because they are educated and not constrained by the lack of choice. They also have far more independence than before...'

The teenage (middle-, as well as working-class) girls knew the family risks they were running. As one of the 15-year-olds put it: 'It would bring too much shame to my family. If they ever found out, they would disown me or send me to a home, I'm sure.'

The system they operate was usually through a male pimp (sometimes these men are also young if worldly-wise students — though full-time pimps are said to go 'talent-scouting' outside school gates, or in discos popular with teenagers). Marina Square and Katong Shopping Centre were two venues used for attracting male clients, and then it was off to one of those cheap short-stay Geylang hotels.

If the men are other students or National Servicemen, the charges ranged from $30–$50 for short-times. Older and better-off men, such as tourists or businessmen, pay up to $300 for overnights with young and fresh 'virgins'. Or, if the girls preferred their 'payment' that way, they'd be taken shopping and have Gucci, Louis Vuitton, Chanel etc treats bought for them.

One explanation offered for this teenage sex-for-sale came from Vincent Lam, of Youth Challenge. He said: 'Singapore youths are very status conscious. They buy branded goods to keep up with an image they have created for themselves in front of their friends.

'But there's a limit to how far their parents will indulge them. So, when luxuries become a habit and the opportunity to make a fast buck presents itself, these kids are most susceptible.

'If they run into debt, they may stupidly turn to loan-sharks. And when they can't make the interest payments, they turn to prostitution...'

R(A) movies: since 1992, adult Singaporeans have enjoyed movies without sex-scene cuts, though interpretations of that 'artistic merit' tag have proved somewhat fluid.

These revelations of teenage part-time prostitutes provoked outpourings of 'Why, Oh Why?' verbal horror among local columnists with over-delicate sensibilities — but the most mature, sensible reaction came from a letter-writer to *The Straits Times*. He urged that Singaporeans should 'learn to lead "simpler" lives, and measure their standard of living not by what we have but by what we are'. Splendid sentiments, but a tall order in madly materialistic money-money modern Singapore. Where 'No money, no honey' is regarded as a clever, cute kind of thing to say...

'She's 13... sells her body for $30'. That was the headline to a splash shock-horror story on *The New Paper*'s front page in July 1995. The teenager had sold herself to a Bangladeshi worker and had sex with him at his Jurong flat, but afterwards the couple were 'spotted' by a suspicious neighbour. In court, the man was sent to jail for six months (a comparatively light sentence, because she had made the first sex-for-money approach).

The teenager was not identified by either name or race but she told the paper she needed the cash for 'cool' things like 'nice dresses' and rollerblades.

She expressed this hope for her future: 'I wish to marry a rich man so I don't have to worry any more. But who will want to marry a girl after she has been accused of being a prostitute?'

More teenage tearaway stories emerged in 1998. One such involved Michelle who run away from home as a 14-year-old and sold herself as a prostitute when she 'fell in love' with a 36-year-old construction worker who'd then introduced her to a pimp. Following which,

COME DEBATE WITH ME, SAYS PM

What some say of Safire debate
/Page 11

WEDNESDAY JULY 19, 1995   MITA (P) 024/04/95   60 CENTS

She's 13
**She's poor.
Like many teens,
she wants to enjoy
the 'cool' things in life.
That leads her to...**

sell her body for $30
/Page 10

Shockingly cool: *The teenager with her $90 pair of Rollerblades which she paid for herself. Her mother said "she would not tell me" where she got the money.*

The New Paper's front pages on teenage sex-for-sale 'part-timers', presented with maximum shock value.

Story that will make you say: Wah lau!

A★ girl, 13, turns KTV hostess
/Page 5

Spice Girl's engagement ring /Page 2

Why shouldn't a 'garang' woman cry? /Page 32

Singapore Press Holdings

she worked in a Geylang brothel where she averaged three men a night at $150 per 30-minute session. Three weeks later, she'd made $5,400 — 25 per cent of which she'd handed over to the pimp, the rest she gave to her boyfriend who said he'd 'look after it' and give her 'pocket money' when she needed it.

Soon afterwards, she was arrested (for not having her ID card) by Anti-Vice police during a Geylang raid and sent to a home for wayward teens. Michelle has not seen her boyfriend since he collected her money, and she was quoted as saying: 'If I didn't prostitute myself, he would have been angry with me. I will be 16 this year, I could have been taking my O-levels. Of course I regret what I've done.'

Michelle's story was soon followed by the splash tabloid treatment given to 'Susan' who had, as a 13-year-old, worked as a karaoke lounge hostess. Susan was academically bright but left school because she found the teaching system 'boring and tiring'. She told a KTV lounge manager she was 18 and got a job there straightaway, soon earning $2,000–$4,000 per month. She described her work: 'Just sit with the men, talk to them and sing with them. Of course, you have to let them touch your shoulder or legs... five hours pass in a blink and you have a few hundred dollars in your hand.' Susan insisted she never did sex or 'extra services' with her karaoke customers — and that she'd stopped her work only because her KJ boyfriend didn't like seeing her fool around with strange men in the lounge.

It should be stressed that these are very much isolated cases rather than growing trends (or anything like the many Japanese schoolgirls who offer their favours to older men for money the girls like to spend on clothes and treats — one such Tokyo schoolgirl was quoted as casually describing her ECA sex-for-sale as 'like any other part-time work — the same as flipping burgers in McDonald's, but better paid').

A locally-conducted lifestyle survey of 5,149 school students aged from 12–19 insisted that 1-in-5 teenaged girls had sex by the age of 19, with only half of them using protection. Of the boys, 1-in-5 also had sex by 19, with many of them starting at 15 and again, with only half using condoms. But the 1995 survey's overall finding was that local school-going teenagers were as wholesome as Singapore would prefer to assume they were.

This was backed up by findings of another survey (published in March 1998) of 400 young people aged between 13 and 19 which found that almost two-thirds of Singapore teenagers did not even date or kiss.

Just 23 of the 400 surveyed said they were no longer virgins, with 12 of these saying they'd sex with more than one partner (two had started at 13 and one girl aged 17 said she'd already had five sex partners).

Some social workers were wary of these face-to-face survey findings, suspecting that the teenagers might have said 'what was expected of them' and that the proportion of teenagers having sex was actually 10–12 percent, rather than the survey's average of six percent. This was taking into account Ministry of Health figures which showed that in 1996, there had been 1,487 abortions among Singapore girls aged between 10 and 19 (averaging out as four per day). While in the same year, there had been two teenage births per day.

An editorial in *The Sunday Times* noted that 'the shyness factor in research surveys about attitudes — which inevitably invite judgments — skewed the data.' The newspaper added: 'But if the data give a true picture, then the old-fashioned should be delighted. Teenagers' values are still the norm, Singapore's youth are not promiscuous…'

MISTRESSES, MODELS AND ACTRESSES

It's not just some teenagers making the sex-equals-cash connection: grown-up 'respectable' women do so also. Such as mistresses, an old-fashioned concept maybe but one still alive in today's Singapore. Such women either get flats bought for them, or are installed in service apartments. For their part, they must be ready, fragrant, powdered and willing whenever the man who paid up can (or wants to) call around to collect some return on his investment. One such mistress was said (by a women's magazine) to earn, so to speak, an annual salary of $40,000 for this novel form of employment.

Of course, gossipy tongues (often female) will always hint that a woman doing well without any apparent self-earned source of income is 'on the game' in some shape or form. How else to explain the rumours about two well-known model agencies which allegedly recruit some of their girls not for the catwalk but for the boudoir? Or those air stewardesses said to be 'available', care of certain upmarket bars and a plush nightclub in a well-known Orchard Road hotel? Or those TV stars who are said to 'go' for $2,000 per overnight?

TCS can be a right hotbed of nasty gossip. When a TCS actress came back from a Hongkong holiday, she found herself (anonymously) accused of being a prostitute while in the colony: this tittle-tattle story was run in the *Lianhe Wanbao* Chinese-language newspaper, without actually naming the actress. The same newspaper also ran a story about 'foreign (female) artistes living in Singapore' who were seen going in and out of hotels, the implication being they were servicing male clients in their hotel bedrooms — but again, no names and no proof.

So it was probably in her best interests that perky ex-TCS actress Jazreel Low went public in 1992 with the astonishing details of an 'offer' that had come her way. Three local businessmen, insisted Jazreel, were prepared to pay a combined total of $1.2 million for her sexual favours. She snapped through *Lianhe Wanbao*: 'I told them that I'm no prostitute, and that I'm not interested in their money.' She also said her then-boyfriend (singer Eric Moo) joked about it: 'He could not see why I was worth so much money!'

BATAM AND BINTAN

Up to 800 Indonesian women are guesstimated to 'work' on Singapore's neighbouring Indonesian islands of Batam and Bintan. These women come from all over Indonesia's sprawling archipelago, drawn to these once-quiet islands by the lure of the mighty Singapore dollar. For, with Batam just 30 minutes and Bintan about an hour away by fast ferry, many Singaporean men come here to enjoy their 'R&R breaks'.

Batam's working women work in different ways, all of which are strictly indoors. Batam's main town of Nagoya has several fishtank-style massage parlours, karaoke and KTV joints, discos, nightclubs, lounges, bars, even ambiguous hair-dressing salons.

Bintan's sex-for-sale is different; more discreet, less pushy. But then, this island does have its extraordinary 'love village' — or 'chicken farm', as it's more crudely known. This is a little settlement, some 17 kilometres out of Bintan's likeable main town Tanjung Pinang. It's inaccessible by anything other than taxis, which wait till their battered cars are filled up with excited men before trundling off into the countryside.

Eventually, they turn off the main road and down a dirt track, go through a manned security barrier — and there it is. A little self-contained village, literally in the middle of nowhere, with scores of awaiting girls offering on-the-spot services or, as they'd prefer, aiming to be taken out to hotels (once 'signing-out' formalities are completed).

Bintan is specially popular with older Singaporean men, who are naturally delighted to have sexually-energetic, often-pretty and always much younger girls paying such attention to them. Or rather, to what's in their wallets. For it's been tagged the 'nasi lemak to go' syndrome. That is, these men are usually over-55 and thus able to withdraw their CPF savings. And when these girls have parted those men from their money, they discard the 'grand-dads' as they would the wrapping on a now-eaten nasi lemak meal.

ORCHID

BECK'S
Imported from Germany

Orchid 99
MASSAGE,
COFFEE HOUSE & PUB
Address : Complex Sejati
Block F No. 46 Home :
Samping Kanan
Batam Jaya Hotel Tel. 459643

CV. NEW BERLIAN BATAM

TRADISIONAL
MASSAGE PARLOUR/
BARBER SHOP
SALON /AMUSEMENT
CENTRE & KARAOKE

Jalan Lubuk Baja I Komplek Sri Jaya
Blok B No. 8, 10,11, 12 Kodya Batam
Tel: 457972

OPEN:
10.00 – 24.00 Local Time
Buka: 10.00 – 24.00 Wib

One WAY
Disco Night Club
Karaoke & KTV Room
Tiger BEER

GOLDEN STAR (88)
BATAM SEJATI
NIGHT CLUB & PUB
COMPLEX SRI JAYA ABACK NO. 11 - 12 - 13 - 14 BATAM ISLAND

Crown MASSAGE TRADISIONAL
Crown Kara Oke

A walk on the wild side: Batam's lively nightlife is pitched mainly at neighbouring Singapore (particularly, its Chinese men). Bintan island next door appeals more to Malay male Singaporeans.

MALE PROSTITUTES

A men-for-men prostitution racket came into the open in late-1997 when a local Chinese man was sentenced to 16 months' jail on charges of abetting 'acts of gross indecency'. He'd run a homosexual brothel where, in the space of two weeks, 34 male clients were 'entertained' by eight male prostitutes (local, Malaysian and one Thai). Police raided the Thomson Road flat after receiving an anonymous tip-off.

The uniquely Singaporean visual stimulation: the swimwear show. The late author and model Bonny Hicks had described these shows as 'the epitome of bad taste... at such close quarters, the men would be looking for that hint of a breast and the women for that imperfect part of the anatomy... 90 percent of the patrons would be male.'

LOOK ☞ 最新录影带出售
UNBEATABLE TITLE & QUALITY

Video movies the censor never saw: handbills like this were once slipped into local letter boxes. In August 1998, some 300,000 mainly porno VCDs were seized and 45 people arrested during island-wide police raids — most of the naughty VCDs were stored at a Yio Chu Kang house.

CHAPTER 3

True Stories

Twelve very different women, but all offering the same 'product' in their various ways. These honest and candid interviews gave the women an opportunity to describe how the world looks from their point of view. Sex-for-sex women are usually not asked how they think, how they feel — only how much they charge.

ESCORT AGENCY
Laura's Story

'I must have earned nearly $100,000 in those two years. In $10,000 banknotes, mainly.'

Seven years ago, at the upscale Orchard Road escort agency she'd just joined, Laura was asked if she wanted a job 'abroad'. Yes, she said quickly. She'd developed a taste for travel. But this particular abroad was not like the usual abroad. It was (let's just say) an oil-rich kingdom in the region.

Laura set off perkily with a girlfriend. On her first visit, she stayed for two weeks. Her girlfriend lasted barely a couple of days, being quickly 'sent back to the shop' for not meeting desired standards. Alone, Laura did two entertainment sessions (no hanky-panky) a day, until a particular prince took a particular liking for her. Laura responded. And more. 'I fell deeply in love with him but, as I told him, I wish he'd been a postman or something — that would have made it easier for me.' Though, of course, a lot less lucrative.

This affair lasted for two-and-a-half years, with Laura quitting her agency after her third visit 'abroad'. As the prince told her: 'I can afford you, so why are you still working when you go back to Singapore?'

It was a period of endless luxury for Laura who, over a space of two years, made nearly 40 visits to the kingdom. She returned to Singapore each time loaded down with cash. Heaps and heaps of it. 'I must have earned nearly $100,000 in those two years. In $10,000 banknotes, mainly.'

She didn't save much, spending lavishly (and carelessly) on friends, on clothes, on expensive fripperies, even on down-and-outs (she once gave $200 to an Indian beggar outside a Shaw Centre boutique, only to be embarrassed by the way he kept bowing to her in stunned gratitude).

Laura's good life came to a sudden end. Through that girlfriend who hadn't lasted long in the kingdom. For she'd clearly been harbouring a deep grudge. A phone call at Laura's Singapore flat. She was out, her (so-called) girlfriend was in. She answered the phone and, in response to his angry questions, she told the suspicious prince that Laura was having an affair on her home patch (true, she was — though it was a mere fling). The next time the now livid prince phoned Singapore, it was Laura's bad luck that a man (not the boyfriend, this one was in fact a gay man pal) answered. That was all the 'evidence' the prince needed. The affair was over.

'I was disappointed, but not heartbroken. I went off travelling — to Europe — with the money I had left until it ran out. Then I came back to Singapore. I was 23. And broke again.'

Laura's line of lucrative work was not the work of fate or destiny, though few would have expected the teenage Laura to end up doing 'that kind of thing'.

A physically attractive Chinese, she was brought up by her granny. Her parents parted while she was a baby. She lived with her mother between the ages of 11 and 14. That is, until mum — a traditional mainland China woman — objected so much to the 'wrong kind of company' she considered her daughter was keeping that she took to locking Laura in the house at night.

They lived in Katong, and it was the Eurasian teenagers (with their more liberal parents) that Laura's mother didn't care much for. For starters, few of the girls were still virgins by their mid-teens. This troubled the young and intact Laura. 'Why not me? Am I ugly? What's wrong with me?' Such were the thoughts that ran through her teenage mind. So, at 15 (her last school year), she made herself 'do it' with a boy — but didn't much enjoy the experience. 'I couldn't understand what the big deal was, or why my friends liked it!'

By the age of 18, a taste for travel was taking her to Malaysia, Thailand, even Australia. But further travel needed further funding. So with her pal, she flicked through the small ads and picked out one for Escort Agencies. They were a naive duo, assuming that escorting simply meant showing foreign tourists around Singapore and getting paid for it.

Laura was genuinely shocked when the agency told her what escorting usually fully involved. But the duo decided they'd try it, and try to avoid the naughty stuff — even if far more calls to the agency were for massage than for escort.

Early one evening, a caller asked for a Chinese girl to do massage. Just Laura and an older Malay woman were on duty. Laura shook her head but the Malay said: 'Don't be silly, just do five minutes *bedek-bedek* (pretend) massage, then talk.'

Besides, it was $60 for an hour. Adopting the as yet uninvented slogan 'Just Do It', Laura set off. 'I had no choice, my money was so low!' — and found that her first-ever client (a Mandarin Hotel guest) was a handsome 32-year-old Japanese businessman.

Laura was nervous, especially when he told her not to bother with a rub — observing that she'd forgotten her oil anyhow (though her worldly-wise Malay colleague had given her condoms). She 'just did it', relieved that he was pleasant and 'no brute'. When he'd finished, he gave her $400 and told her to leave immediately.

Outside, Laura gulped the Orchard Road late afternoon air. 'I felt horrible inside. I felt I'd created the biggest shame of my life. And I felt I'd definitely never do it again.'

She went straight home, avoiding the agency. There, the implications of those $400 loomed larger and larger.

And so, the next day (for once, not worrying about whether she could splash out on a taxi to work), she'd made up her young mind. She told her boss she would do massage. And yes, sex.

'Soon, I was the most popular girl! I was the youngest, and Chinese men seem to like the young, fresh bodies of innocent, green girls. They certainly pay more for that.'

Two months after this major career move, Laura upgraded to a more swish escort agency and worked there every night for three months. The basic money deal was now a $400 package for two hours (with extras), of which $100 went to the agency. 'I was getting a lot of calls asking for me by name and soon I had thousands in the bank, hundreds in my pocket. I wanted more!'

She became pro-active and, when she could, 'headhunted' her own clients. Mainly by working on the agency switchboard and *choping* those who didn't haggle about price over the phone. For nine months, Laura took on three or four jobs a day (clearing a daily $1,000 easily) before calling it a day. 'At that age, you can keep up the pace.'

She was also spending heavily. A lot went on medical bills to ensure she maintained her much-sought-after fresh young complexion and fragrant, flawless body. Then, she'd spend from $500–$1,500 on clothes without a second thought — but usually received a discount, as she always paid in cash.

Her mother? 'She didn't know. I'd moved out long before and was putting up with a girlfriend.' The travel bug struck her again, and during one such trip she started an affair with a man in Kuala Lumpur. 'I had so much spare cash, he thought I was from a well-off family! I told him my dad was rich, and indulgent.'

Now keenly aware of her earning power and 'market value', Laura upgraded yet again — to a top-of-the-line Orchard Road escort agency. Which is where she got her first call to work 'abroad'.

These days? Now her high life is so well and truly over? Laura is quiet, reflective, almost demure. 'I don't really want to work in this line any more. Besides, I'm 28 now — and the other working girls are so much younger. I'm pretty sure I can survive on a normal salary, so I've gone back to school to study something useful.

'I still have an agent, who fixes me up with clients from time to time. They're usually local, Chinese and youngish. We go night-clubbing, entertaining only. I get $150 for a session but most times I don't do sex any more. Besides, karaoke makes escort work so much easier — all they want to do is drink and sing with pretty, sweet companions alongside them, praising their voices.

'Over the last five years since my big affair ended, I've done sex for money only about 20 times. Sometimes, if I've liked the man, I charged $300. But usually, it's $400 and up. For a short time, no overnights.

And no funny stuff, just straight sex. Always with a condom, too.

'Besides, it's so much trouble looking good, dressing up, entertaining. Just too much effort. But mind you, for $400, I'd still make that effort.'

Her mother? She knows now, all right. She's known for a good few years what her daughter Laura did — and at times still does — to earn big money. They don't talk much about it. They don't talk about much at all. Their relationship is not a close one. It never really was...

Sex itself doesn't mean much these days to Laura, either. She has sex, all right — for fun, to relieve her itch — two or so times a month, and usually with a younger man. 'They're very quick and I climax very fast, often before them. Older men don't like women saying "Hurry up", do they? Anyway, when it's me who wants the sex, I don't get paid!'

Laura insists she does enjoy the sweet sensation of falling in love, that whole romantic early bit — and the first few bouts of sex with a new man. 'But I soon get bored and it ends — and I don't seem to really care. I think I must have a male attitude to sex, no?'

Then Laura sighs, quietly: 'Maybe it's fated that I'm alone now. Maybe, I always will be. Yet, yes I would like to be normal, have a husband, child and all that. But I fear it's all a bit too late for me now. Anyhow, I don't think a Singapore man would have me now, if he knows what I used to do. It won't happen, I'm pretty sure.'

LOUNGE HOSTESS
Carolina's Story

'Some men even expect you to play with their things, while they sip their drinks.'

The traditional lounge — where charming, elegant hostesses sit and chat with male guests while sex is — officially — off the menu, is in its death throes in Singapore. There are still some around town, catering to locals and Westerners alike. But they're being squeezed out by Japanese lounges, Chinese nightclubs, karaoke lounges and those so-dark, high-chaired music lounge joints.

The old-style lounges almost evoke an earlier era, when women 'companions' were valued for their grace and conversational skills, rather than their sexual availability. Which is not to say sex does not ensue after an evening spent in a lounge with a hostess. It's just that hanky-panky isn't supposed to happen in the lounge itself, where the house rule is usually 'no nonsense here'. But waiters will, upon discreet request, discreetly point out to a male guest towards which girls 'do it in their own time, it's between you two, sir'.

There are three such old-style lounges around United Square. Carolina works at one, six nights a week from 5 pm to 1 am. She's an English-educated Chinese divorcee with one child, 28 years of age, and an elegant, charming woman. As are most of the 20-odd other hostesses in the lounge because, says Carolina, the no hanky-panky house rule means the 'nicer sort of girl' works there. For if a boozed-up guest does get too frisky with a hostess, she can summon the manager who will sternly tell him: 'This is a lounge, not a bar' — and ask him to leave if he's not prepared to stop acting the *cheeko*.

Carolina worked before in a Japanese lounge. There are now at least 15 of these around town and though they were originally set up by Japanese men to emulate the Tokyo style of hostess nightclub, it's mainly Chinese handphone-toters who fill them out these nights.

In these joints, almost anything goes. They're expensive, for a start. It usually costs $40 per hour to hire a chosen girl (Japanese lounges prefer to employ Chinese) to sit and whatever with a male guest. She gets (usually) $25 of that, plus commission on drinks bought under her 'influence' — with the jackpot hit if a $750 bottle of premium brandy gets cracked open by her male guest. On basic salary alone, hostesses in Japanese lounges can earn up to $3,000 a month, plus of course all those extras. But at a price...

Carolina: 'I couldn't stick it there after six months and had to leave, despite the good money. For a start, before you get the job, you've got to show the management you can look very sexy. You're not allowed to wear pants (in her current job, she prefers to wear tailored trousers), and your skirts or dresses must be either very short or must have a long slit to show off all your leg. And your breasts mustn't look too covered up. Your style of dressing and approach to the guests must suggest your accessibility, availability and your sex appeal...

'You can't choose your guest. He tells the Mummy who he wants, and she's sent to him. It's darker in

Japanese lounges, and some men even expect you to play with their things while they sip their drinks. They're very gropey-gropey, and feel the girls all over as and when they want to. She's not expected to complain, or she'll be sent back to the Mummy.

'They can book you out during lounge hours or afterwards for all-nights. Pretty much every girl is for hire and although you can refuse to go with a man you really don't like, if you turn too many down, you'll probably lose your job. Not that most of the girls objected anyhow, because the money is so good — and you can see many of the girls driving happily around town in nice cars of their own. Sometimes, the girls can even find a high-earning husband through their work at the lounge and they can stop working.

'Naive girls wouldn't last long at a Japanese lounge. I left not because I'm prim but because I got fed up with all that groping in the dark and going with men I really didn't like.'

Now at her non-Japanese lounge, Carolina can pick which men — if any — she'll see more of after work. That's two at the most in an average week. She prefers to go out on the town first, going with the man to clubs such as Top Ten, then maybe enjoying an early morning meal at Newton Circus before finally getting down to business.

That way, it seems like she's out on a date rather than working. What's more, Carolina would rather not ask the man outright for the money she expects for her sexual favours, although she'd raise hell if she didn't get a morning-afterwards tip of at least $250. This financial coyness also helps her not to think of herself as a prostitute. Her all-night rate at the Japanese lounge, by the way, was at least $350.

At her 'no hanky-panky' lounge, the most unpleasantness comes between the girls themselves, if they argue over who's entitled to which tips. Each hostess can work up to three tables, hopping around to keep the various men happy. If she finds another girl nipping into a seat she's just vacated — and thereby establishing her claim to a tip — that's when fur can fly. Sometimes real catfights with glasses flying can break out between arguing girls (adding to the lounge entertainment for male onlookers?).

When a particular table asks for the drinks bill, the red LED display sign over the entrance door usually saying 'Welcome' changes to give that table's number (T4, etc). The girls rarely lose sight of — or forget about — that signboard. Alongside me, when two hair-permed Chinese handphone-toters called for the bill, they were overwhelmed within a minute by no less than six squealing girls. By what I could see, each of these girls (all Chinese, in those chiffon-style songbird outfits) was getting a $50 note slipped either down her bosom or into her eager hand.

If a hostess thinks a guest looks like an above-average big-spender prospect, she'll stick with just that one man and act touchy-touchy, stroky-stroky sexy with him. A lounge waiter indicated to me that one particularly alluring Malay hostess (who was doing just that with a guest) was one of those girls who 'do it', and that if I really wanted, he could lure her away to tend to me. I reluctantly declined the offer. Reluctantly, because that hostess looked a real steamy firecracker

— whereas Carolina was elegant, stylish, even a little too demure.

Even more so, as if she had just come from her CBD executive desk, was Suzanna. She slipped into the seat alongside me during a prolonged absence by Carolina. 'I don't like to see a charming man being left alone — may I?' she sighed charmingly.

Suzanna, a 31-year-old Eurasian and another divorcee (she'd married at 18), was not long for the lounge. For she'd already hooked her big fish. He was (she said) a quiet, middle-aged Belgian man, soon to return to Europe after his spell of work duty in Singapore. She'd met him at the lounge, and was convinced she'd be joining him in Europe on a permanent basis — once he'd sorted out the awkward little problem of his current wife back home.

But Suzanna continued her 'no hanky-panky' hostessing at the lounge. She said she enjoyed the company of men, she liked being with them and chatting to them. Besides, the work 'helped to pass the time'. She only worked part-time there, starting at 9 pm, and was thus not on a salary but tips only.

She quickly left the seat next to me when Carolina loomed into view over her, giving her a most menacing look…

GEYLANG'S BROTHEL LAND
Rani's Story

'I don't like doing sex at all — but I can
pretend real good, yes?'

You can book Rani's services through most of Geylang's licensed brothels. But she does have a favourite cathouse: 'It's new, very clean, even a bit romantic.' In between two of Geylang's 'busiest' lorongs, it's a modern three-storey town house — much like the type you see advertised for well over $1 million. Only in the attic of this one is a most unusual, complicated-looking chair — a cross between those plush gym devices jocks exercise in, and a dentist's chair. Rani calls this unique item of Geylang furniture the 'f*cking chair'.

For, with a few deft turns of its side-handles, Rani — not a small woman — can nimbly climb onto this chair and give its awaiting male occupant a 'workout' that reaches the parts most gym exercises miss.

With or without a 'f*cking chair', this brothel has a distinct edge over Geylang's longer-established institutions. From outside, its classy coloured neon lights give it the look of a good motel or a US-style diner. Inside, the reception foyer is plush, with little jokes like a bowl with Ria condoms at the booking desk (the way other joints might have boiled sweets).

Virtually all the faces inside are Chinese, including the good-looking women who in their ornamental cheongsams act as 'greetesses'. The waiting area is civilised, with choice of tea or coffee (no booze and no gambling, by law, allowed). Plus an unusually interesting choice of reading material (not the usual doctor's waiting room fare), while you wait.

Upstairs, all the bedrooms are different, especially with their main items — king-sized beds. One is circular, another is mounted, all are plush; it could even be a furniture store's beds display section. All the bedrooms have large mirrors around their walls, and on their ceilings, which makes them seem huge. And Rani goes more eagerly to this cathouse than to others when her pager flashes up its number.

Some Geylang bordellos may be old and uncomfortable, but the price for Rani's services is the same at them all — with or without an unusual chair.

She costs between $100 and $150 for a short time (effectively 30 mins) — or Class C and B, respectively. On the Geylang scale, Class A commands $200, while there's an unofficial Class D (its women are usually over 40) charging down to even just $50. No matter what their good looks, age or figure, girls can also be 'downgraded' if they have given birth. Male customers think that their vaginas have a greater 'elasticity' and are therefore less appealing than those of women who have not had a child.

Rani falls short of Geylang's Class A, whose girls are virtually all Chinese, pretty and under 30. As Rani says: 'I'm too dark, too fat for Class A.'

She's Indian, and 26 years old. She takes bra size 36in/93cm, C Cup, and her tummy and thighs are in proportion to this top-end ampleness. Indians or *ang mohs* don't always regard her as 'too fat': indeed, many of her 15 or so regulars ask for her because she's what they regard (and enjoy) as 'voluptuous'. But local Chinese male tastes prefer their girls to be downright slim, as young and 'virginal' as they can find them — and usually, Chinese.

Of a $100 fee, Rani gets $44. The rest is divided between her boss and the cathouse in which she conducts that particular assignment. Her busiest days can involve up to eight clients, while her average is five. She is 'on duty' from 12.30 pm to midnight, six days a week. Sundays are days off; she needs the rest, as she says, 'especially down there'.

What does Rani unveil for her clients? In Geylang, there's almost a Standard Operating Procedure (SOP) with yellow card girls and certainly with Rani. With first-time callers, there's an 'introduction' in the waiting room, when either side can back out of the deal.

If all seems OK, it's cash in advance and off to a private, locked-door air-con room. No tantalising striptease or 'let's get to know each other' non-essential conversation: the girl strips off straightaway, and takes the man into the shower. There he's given a head-to-toe clean-up, with particular emphasis on what's between his legs (this allows the girl to also check for visible signs of sexual ill-health).

Straight onto the bed, and straight on with a condom (on the house). Rani calls the next stage 'sucking my ice cream', the meaning of which should be fairly plain. Then, as quickly as gives no offence, she goes to the 'main course'. Most girls try to make this pass as rapidly as possible. The favoured technique is to come on strong with 'excited' moans and groans, and little thrilling phrases like 'You feel so good, darling' or 'I like a strong man like you, my love' — and so on. Such potentially Oscar-winning acting performances usually work. The girl has conducted her task speedily, and the man feels his sexual ego has been well massaged.

Literally within seconds of matters having come to a head, the girl is back on her feet, heading for the shower unit again, and turning on all the lights as brightly as possible — adhering to the fast food industry principle of garish illumination to encourage customers not to linger when they've finished their meal? The man will then be directed to the shower unit for a solo wash. When he comes out again, the girl is usually already applying the final face make-up touches to her fully-dressed self. The whole SOP should last no more than 30 minutes, maximum.

Rani is better than most at the fake sexually passionate routine. For she really doesn't like her work, not one little bit. 'I don't like doing sex at all — but I pretend real good, yes?'

She's in it for the money, of course. It was the obvious, easiest way she could think of to raise a tidy sum of capital in the shortest time. She tried being a lounge hostess, but the pay was largely tips-based. So she'd been on the Geylang game for eight months, and planned to quit when a year was up. That gave her a feasible deadline which helped when she didn't want to think about what she was doing while she was doing it — which was usually always.

Rani saves most of her money, with her one notable indulgence being her $70 hairdos. She gets as angry if a man tries to touch her thickly sprayed hair as she does if the man tries to kiss her on the lips (Geylang girls don't go in for mouth-to-mouth kissing), and will scold the man.

The men who distress her the most are those US Navy clients who get sent her way, especially the black ones (such men are directed to her as in the mainly Chinese cathouses of Geylang, she speaks English better than most). 'They're so big, and their cocks can hurt. They're so tough too. They squeeze and grab and punch my tits. They want to turn me over to make love through the back door way. They like to do the rough stuff that they do with girls in Thailand, like sticking their fingers up my bum which really does hurt.

'If they go on top of me, they're so heavy and I have to keep saying "faster, faster" to make them come quicker, so I can get out from under them. Sometimes, I can hardly breathe!

'And a lot of them drink too, so their breath smells bad. Now I try to avoid *mat sallehs* like them, I just don't want their business...'

Rani is Singaporean, but most of her family are now in Malaysia. If she does build up good money from what she hopes will be her short career in Geylang, she expects to move to Malaysia (the nature of her Singapore career is not known there, her family think she's working in a plush hotel and sharing a flat with other 'decent' girls). There, she hopes to be able to start her own small business — a market stall or some such.

That's the good news. The bad news is that many young women went into Singapore's sex-for-sale line of work, intending it to last just a year or two — enough, they thought, to raise a tidy sum of (tax-free) money to bale out again on the financial up.

But many years later, many of them are still there, still at it. Possibly downgraded to that Class D category, or plying their trade in the dank lanes off Desker Road. Where they face an extremely uncertain — and probably dismal — future...

THE MEDIUM IS THE MASSAGE
Ria's Story

'I know what men are like,
sometimes they get excited.'

'Stand Up For Singapore' — that's one of Ria's little jokes as she offers her 'extra services' to men at the massage salon where she works. She giggles too when she tags the masculine focus of her extra services as 'your little brother — it goes with you everywhere you go!' Then afterwards, Ria says (with a broad smile): 'Thank you for coming!' You'd think Ria enjoys her work. By and large, she does...

Ria has been massaging for a living for nearly a year, six days (11 am–7 pm) a week at a West Coast health centre which offers steam bath and sauna as well as massage. Hers is a proper massage, using her own Revlon 'very cooling and relaxing' body lotion — unlike most other masseuses who are better at the 'extra services' than at the actual massaging.

For Ria went for proper massage instruction ($250 for a three-week course), after she decided she didn't like the Japanese lounge where she'd worked for a year: 'Sometimes, it was so naughty there.' It was her marriage breakdown (no children) that propelled her initially into this line of business: 'I started smoking and drinking, being naughty in all sorts of ways.' Before then, as a married woman, she'd held down a decent but low-paying job at an Orchard Road hotel.

As a masseuse, Ria's sole 'extra service' is a handjob. She won't do anything else: 'Only my right hand is naughty now.' No lovemaking, no stripping, no home visits — just masturbation alone.

That's only partly because registered massage salon/health centre laws are specific. Under the Massage Establishment Act 1959, all male clients must enter their name and ID/passport number into the reception desk book. Most give fictitious details with the receptionists sometimes saying, if a man looks uneasy about giving his particulars: 'Anything, lah!'

No monkey business at all is supposed to take place within the premises. All cubicle doors must remain unlocked, and male clients are asked not to make any noise (the only sound that should legally be heard is that 'clap-clap' of massaging hands).

Ria's form of extra service is the usual massage salon limit — and only, technically, upon request. Most men do request. Indeed, they'd be surprised if no such service is suggested to them during or after their massage. Some of the less swish massage joints are not so particular about what their girls do, including lovemaking (even behind unlocked cubicle doors).

But in Ria's case, she says she knows of toilers in her trade being trapped by undercover (or should that be uncovered?) officials testing a joint's legitimacy, then prosecuting the girl and sometimes even having the whole place temporarily shut down.

So, in the case of first-time clients, Ria doesn't even hint at any extras being on offer. If he asks, she'll re-ply she doesn't do that kind of thing — she specialises in 'really good' massages alone. Only her regulars, those she trusts or likes, get asked: 'Will there be anything else, sir?'

Her health centre charges $32 per one-hour (more like 45 mins) massage, while Orchard Road salons tend to charge $50. Of this, Ria gets $11 massage fee. She pockets all the 'extra' fees; in her case, that's a no-haggle charge of $50 per hand-job.

Most of her customers are 'educated Chinese'. She defines this category by the fact that they don't have tattoos on their bodies. Those that do, she doesn't like. 'They are rough, they grab my tits, they're like animals. I won't do them.' As an English-speaking Malay, the few Caucasians that turn up at the salon are allocated to her.

Ria makes her extra service sound almost like a therapeutic measure. 'As I massage men, I can see what they're like, they get excited. Very excited. But after I handle their "little brother", they're calm and relaxed again.'

Ria does actually like men, unlike many other masseuses who regard them only as 'punters'. But as for her own urges, she has that widespread Singaporean female belief that recreational sex is something only men engage in, not women. 'I don't have sex for fun. I take medicine to cool me down — jamu from Indonesia. But sometimes, yes, I use this.' She wiggled the middle finger of her right hand.

Now 29 and a fine-looking (shapely, too) woman, Ria lives with her sister in Jurong and spends most nights not being a bad girl but merely watching videos (and taking her jamu?). Her ultimate aim is a modest one.

'I hope I'll meet a good, hard-working man who doesn't drink, doesn't gamble. Then I'd happily become a good housewife. And no more naughty...'

DESKER ROAD
Marja's Story

*'I like to do f*ck-f*ck very quick,*
two minutes is very good.'

Desker Road operates on the high-turnover, low-margin principle. Effectively it's the end of the line for working women in physical decline, or who didn't (or couldn't) save enough money during their prime working years — or who failed to get out while there was still time to try something else, to be someone else...

For after Desker Road, there can surely be very little. The women who work here know they're now hardly going to find that man who will take them away from it all.

There are about 90 back doors in this narrow alleyway, opening up on parlours where the women sit in baby-san cane chairs — which in turn lead to shophouse-length corridors, off which are the cubicles. There's an average of four women per parlour. They do not solicit, they just sit there awaiting visual 'goods on offer' inspection by men 'shoppers'. If a man decides he wants some action, he must step inside and negotiate the deal. Most of the time, the women watch TV, knit, stitch, doze or simply stare back blankly at the entirely male world outside their back doors.

Marja operates in one parlour with four other Malaysian Malays, who look younger and prettier compared to most other Desker Road women. They each commute every day from JB, doing 'shifts' of up to 12 hours for six days a week.

Marja talks about her work as if it were part of the fast-food industry: 'I like to do f*ck-f*ck very quick. Two minutes is very good. And five minutes is the most I like a man to take to make his water come out.'

She charges $40, of which $10 goes to the house, and she wants the money before anything happens. She indicates with a crude two-hand gesture exactly what she does for $40, and laughs.

'I had an American *mat salleh* who did feel-feel, kiss-kiss with me. Then in three minutes, he makes his water before he can f*ck-f*ck! A good customer!'

But there again: 'There was a Chinese man who had drunk much beer comes in with me, we take clothes off, and he goes asleep for 15 minutes! In the end, I just used my hand on him...'

Some customers are rough, too rough. 'An Indian man squeezed my tits so hard, I still have bruises. I cried out, I was very sore — and so I hit him in the face with my fist, like this. Before he could hit me back, I called out for help and two men came quickly to the door, then threw him out. He'd been drinking a lot of beer too.'

Marja is now 33, and has had two husbands (one child). She's been reporting for duty at Desker Road for just over a year. She stays with her family in JB, where her brother is a teacher. 'He says I'm no good, because I do f*ck-f*ck. But I give good money to our family, and I need it for my little girl.'

Marja takes her clients into one of the half-small bedroom width booths, where there is just a single bed (no sheet, a towel only on the plastic mattress), a tap and small sink, lots of toilet paper rolls, many Use Condoms posters on the walls and an inefficient old air-con machine plus fan.

It's not a nice-looking room at all, equipped merely with the bare essentials for the activity that takes place inside it. Marja responds to the posters all over Desker Road, and insists that clients use condoms. If they don't carry them, they must pay $3 for a house condom. She douches herself before and after her business, using a small hose attached to the tap.

With her rapid turnover (she doesn't go in for any sex-play and straightaway pulls her client on top of her — she just lies there and makes herself available) and her more pro-active approach to potential clients (she'll call out to passing men, while most other Desker Road women simply sit and wait), Marja can happily get through up to 10 men in a single shift — though her average is six. One particularly hard-working single session involved 14 men. This was during the last year-end period, and Marja thinks that work bonuses meant more men went 'out to play'.

She has already also won a reputation, it seems, as being 'understanding' as far as fresh young National Service men are concerned. Indeed, guys bringing their 'virgin soldier' NS comrade to Desker Road for 'servic-ing' has achieved a male coming-of-age ritual status locally.

For Marja, it all adds up to good money to bring

back to JB, and so she expects she'll be working at Desker Road for many years to come. And then? Marja would rather not even think about it...

HOUSEWIVES FOR HIRE
Yati's Story

*'Where got free f*ck? Where does that get me?*
If I'm making love to other men,
I'm a businesswoman...'

Yati could simply stay at home in Tampines, looking after her two early-teenage children and tending to the needs of the man who's currently living with her. But her children are independent-minded and out a lot 'in bad company' (which worries Yati). And her ex-husband doesn't give her any money, while her live-in companion doesn't give her as much money as she thinks he should (which annoys Yati). What's more, she gets bored being at home night after night. Just sitting on her assets...

She likes to go out, into town with her girlfriend — and to have a good time. Yati likes her fun, she likes to dance and flirt with men and hear some loud dance music. But nights out in Orchard Road, or any part of town, mean money. And money Yati is short of. But money Yati knows how to get hold of. She reaches for her phone.

She has a choice of five phone numbers. At the receiving end of each should be a man with whom Yati has had sex before. For money, and for fun. Strictly in that order. Her philosophy: 'You give men your body, but not your heart.'

Now 36, Yati knows time is not on her side and that hard living has taken its toll on her looks. But she's still in good shape, she has a winning head of long, flowing hair — and she's 'very good' at doing sex. That's because she herself enjoys a naughty romp; she doesn't just 'make herself available' for a man while she mentally switches off and dreams of TV drama serial plotlines or thinks that the ceiling needs a new coat of paint or whatever.

She gives her men an entertaining time, arousing them with sexual tricks and the arts of love she's picked up over the years — and with which many younger working girls wouldn't even think of bothering. Such fruits of experience give Yati her competitive edge, and are why her regulars are usually happy to hear her sultry voice at the other end of their phones, making an indecent proposal.

Yati's formal line of work over the years has mainly involved waitressing at pubs, bars and clubs. She's always been popular with male customers as she flirts with them (she enjoys male company) as she brings their booze, and always makes time for a friendly chat. Which the men customers like but which the bar managers often don't. Yati has walked out of two waitressing jobs after being scolded by (Chinese) bosses who thought she was enjoying herself too much and not working hard enough.

It was in the mid-1980s at Geylang's Gay World Datoh Rajah (a huge, mainly-Malay/Indonesian nightclub, mysteriously burnt down in October 1992 but now rebuilt) that Yati spent her best — as in, most financially rewarding — waitressing years. She was one of the most popular serving girls there, and she was happy to go off afterwards 'as a businesswoman' with male customers she found appealing — and who were generous with their tips.

But when Yati had to finally stop working at Datoh Rajah (for reasons she's reluctant to spell out), financial realities meant she had to revise her approach to sex and become more hardheaded and calculating, even if she did still enjoy her sex. Alternating between factory jobs ('boring, tiring, low-pay') and waitressing at bars such as those frequented by many Caucasians at Paramount Hotel's pub alley shopping centre off East Coast Road, Yati found ways of letting likely looking customers know that she had things other than Anchor, Tiger or Guinness beers on offer...

'I could have just gone with them for fun, and hoped for more "tips". But, where got free f*ck? Where does that get me? Now I'm a businesswoman! I've got what they want and if they're willing to pay me for it, no problem!' Yati will only go to hotel rooms or private apartments, and aims to come out again $150 richer — though she'd prefer $200.

'Men would invite me to go into town with them for a night out, drinking, disco-dancing and that. I like drinking and I like going out, but then I think — why spend all that money on beer and that when they could just give me that money for having sex? Anyway, after a night drinking, they'd always expect to have sex with me. And where got free f*ck? I get no money for it that way, only a headache the next morning! I'd rather use the money spent on me for myself, to do what I'd like with it.'

Yati doesn't have quite so much fun at all these days — or nights. The man who's moved in with her won't let her work at any job, and threatens to hit her if he thinks she's even just talking with other men. And he can get violent when he gets back after a night's drinking. Yati has to use all sorts of excuses (usually involving female neighbours) to get out of the house for short-time visits to those men who appreciate the sexual skills she unveiled for them after a night's pub waitressing.

One neighbour in particular is helpful in providing a convincing alibi for Yati. That's because she does much the same kind of thing herself. Julie, a 31-year-old and also Malay, works in an Orchard Road boutique during the days — and gets bored out of her skull. But the job, tedious though she finds it, provides her with a solid local cover story to disguise her part-time night work.

So much so that Julie has found herself almost hooked on the dangerous thrills and spills it offers. She does short-times and overnights, in 'nice' hotels (not Geylang-style joints) or private apartments. She sells her sexual attention to men she has met either on fishing trips to Orchard Road discos or bars. She has a strict rule, though. For repeat visits, men can only contact her through a pager. Otherwise, they must wait for her to call them, digging into her informal database.

But if her men are not available when she calls (sometimes, a wife answers and Julie has to quickly put the phone down or say: 'Sorry, wrong number') or if her pager doesn't flash up a number on an evening when she's looking for work, she's prepared to hotfoot down to the Orchard Towers area and see who she can find. She'll aim to keep to her quoted rate of $200 for all-night, but will drop to $150 if it's after midnight and her options look limited.

Julie doesn't desperately need the money. For, although she's separated from her husband, there was no child from the marriage and she can support herself. But Julie, who describes herself as a 'modern Malay', likes to buy nice clothes and things and couldn't afford them from her daytime job's pay. Now her younger sister has expressed an interest in her sideline and has even gone along with Julie a couple of times and sat quietly reading a magazine outside the bedroom while her sister does her business inside. By now, this sister may well have 'graduated' into solo working visits herself.

Besides, Julie enjoys sex with good-looking men or with men she's come to know. She happily talks about how she does it, detailing her favourite sexual positions. Such as squatting over the man, on her feet with her knees bent, facing him: 'That way, I'm in charge — and I can please myself, too.'

The obvious risks of her unorthodox hobby do not worry her overmuch. Plus, Julie is a bit blur at times and, in an almost Freudian way, can make unnecessary problems for herself. Or rather, for her clients. In one man's apartment she left her belt behind and in another's, she forgot to take back with her the panties in which she had arrived (she always carries a spare pair in her bag). These are of course the kind of things an outraged wife notices, if the erring husband doesn't spot them first!

Julie — a woman with sexually attractive looks, plus an enticing bosom — got into this line of work through a Chinese taxi-driver who volunteered the information while she travelled in the back of his cab that she could make a lot of extra money by 'sleeping with *ang mohs*'. He would take a cut, so would a pimp, if she agreed. He left a phone number with her.

She thought about it for a few days, then phoned him and met the Chinese pimp — who already had 12 girls working for him. After a few months, Julie found she could hack the work but not the 50 percent the pimp demanded from her earnings. So, she went freelance. And, at present, she has no plans to retire.

Both Yati and Julie know that the naughty stuff they do now represents no long-term life strategy. But they prefer to simply not think about it, and just see what happens. Tomorrow can take care of itself. For today, there is easy money to be made from men they usually like. And maybe even some enjoyable sex along the way...

ORCHARD ROAD PATROL
Annie's Story

'They pay well and they come quick.'

I met her well after midnight along Orchard Road, near The Promenade. It was about 1.30 am and though she looked a tired woman, Annie was trying hard to solicit me. There weren't many other people around, so I guess I was about her last hope for that night.

Instead, we sat on a roadside seat and we chatted. For about an hour, Annie was that chatty. We talked about the old walk-up flat she shared, off nearby Killiney Road. How she could use it for work purposes only late at night because the bathroom was in a shared area and she didn't want her flatmates to bump into her male 'friends'. So she had to keep the noise down in her room and she'd have BBC World Service radio on nonstop to drown out any unavoidable sounds. If she could bring a guy back there, she'd aim at $150 for a short time and $200 for till morning.

She was so chatty sitting there, she even told me about her washing machine, an Elba. I'd got just one myself and what a coincidence, we agreed. We both thought our Elbas had a long wash cycle, taking almost an hour. Then it hit me. There I was sitting on Orchard Road about two in the morning, sharing a seat with a hooker who now-and-then reminded me of the titillating erotic excitements that could be mine for a discounted price — and there we were, swopping notes on goddam washing machines?

I met Annie a few times after that, in daylight and over chatty coffees. Not so often, because she had a daytime job in an off-Orchard hotel's massage salon. Though she didn't get much work there, she had to be on-call for long hours most days of the week. At this salon, she would offer customers the choice of a proper, expert massage with body lotion — or a sexy version, where her fingers would gently flit butterfly-style all over his body in a teasing way. She'd happily take most of her clothes off for this, and add to the fun with brushes of a body-on-body massage. And yes, she was prepared to make love with a man in the salon, once she'd got to know him. Which often meant by the time of his second visit requesting her in particular, as she welcomed the extra money that went straight into her wallet. Which was why she moonlighted on Orchard Road, the money was all hers...

Annie had efficiently built-up a small database of known clients who could contact her by pager or handphone. They tended to be Caucasians who liked her good if somewhat singsong English, which she said she'd learned back home in Vietnam before coming to Singapore.

She also liked Japanese guys because 'they pay well and they come quick'. These tended to be tourists rather than expats — and Annie tracked them down by daylight along Orchard Road, using the lingering eye-contact tactic. Such Japanese men were happy to meet her charges — $250 per short-time, $400 all-night (gullibles she'd try to hit for her jackpot price of $500). These all-nighters also meant Annie could enjoy a night in an upscale Orchard Road hotel bedroom far nicer than hers at home, and she could take away a handy stock of hotel toiletries to brighten up her bathroom cabinet.

Annie was well-versed in the layouts of big hotels and could breeze in and out of them as if she were a hotel guest, and not a hustler trying to work out where the hell his room number was located. Her dress style helped with this — she was never showy or sexy-looking in how she appeared (though in her wardrobe, she had outfits that could tempt a monk) and to hotel security guards, she probably looked like an efficient modern businesswoman (which, in a sense, she was).

Annie did have occasional difficulties in Orchard Road hotels. In one, a Chinese security guard nabbed her in an upstairs corridor after he'd spotted her on video looking for her client's room. She dealt with his threats by giving him a hand-job in his security office while his colleague went out for a coffee. In another hotel, she'd been stopped at the lift by a Malay security guard who insisted on a freebie before he'd let her go. Annie didn't specify how she'd responded, though she insisted he'd had 'a tiny cock'.

As with Chinese guys, Annie could put on a passion-show for Japanese clients and play so skilfully with his dick before actually doing the business, that it would be all over within two minutes. Literally all over, for Annie knows what hookers know. That as soon as a client has come, he wants her to disappear and quick — so she'd be washed and dressed before he'd even finished his post-coital cigarette, dispensing with any after-sales service, and well before he started wanting an action replay. When Annie described a client as 'a very good lover', that's what she meant — he came quickly. She shuddered when recalling a German client. He'd kept it up and in her for an hour, leaving her rather tired and very sore.

To add to her working skills, Annie was street-smart with a good nose for avoiding trouble. She once abandoned a Caucasian customer because she didn't like the way while in a cab heading for his East Coast apartment, he kept grabbing her tits and slipping his hand up her skirt. She never lip-kissed, she examined men's dicks for their state of personal health/hygiene (not obviously, she'd disguise it as sexual play-play). She always carried condoms (her favourite brand being Durex Featherlite). And sometimes, all else being equal, she could herself enjoy the sex. She'd even suggest different ways of doing so, such as a doggie-paddle — for which she had a soft spot (though she was once scolded by a guy for watching the TV and letting her mind drift away from the business in hand).

Annie might not be the sexiest-looking working girl in town, but she looked well and was in good body-shape for a woman in her early thirties. But above all, she left her good clients feeling well-serviced and even with the impression that she'd enjoyed it too.

Annie knew the smart bars for fishing trips. Dress up smartly and try The Raffles' Long Bar, Captain's Bar at The Oriental, Marina Mandarin's Cricketers Bar and the hotel bars at Ana and Shangri-La. She also preferred to fish alone. She did once hook up with a Thai girl but as she was younger with a sweet face and long flowing hair, Annie found herself picking up the crumbs (and the crumb-bums). Her Thai partner-in-crime refused to do all-nights for less than $300 and Annie didn't like that 'I'm the cut-price deal' feeling. Sometimes with her no-haggling stance, the Thai girl wouldn't get any business at all — and so might work the early-bird shift in Geylang. This meant hitting the (usually Chinese) factory guys between 4–5 am before they started work, and doing 15-minute quickies in alleyways for $50 a go. Then with her $200, she would sleep all day. Annie herself never chose to join her colleague on these pre-dawn last-ditch sessions.

Nor did she work the well-known pick-up bars of

Orchard Towers or along Scotts Road, though she was always hearing stories from such joints. Like, about the seemingly well-endowed Thai girl who under pressure from a bear-hug by a muscular US Navy shore-leave sailor felt one of her silicone implants leaking so painfully, she had to be rushed to a nearby A&E hospital.

Not that Annie always had things all her own way. She told me about one particular night-of-mishaps. With her scorecard blank, she'd gone to Orchard Towers for the 2–3 am flush-out period, when guys stagger out full of booze and not knowing what's going on. Annie hooked one, a Japanese guy, and got him to buy a quickie at her place for $150. However, when they'd got there and he'd found her room to be well below Japanese bedroom standards, he sobered up and insisted he'd pay only $80.

Annie refused and demanded he return her to Orchard Towers while it still had business opportunities. Back there at 3 am, she found a sozzled Indian man who took her to a nearby carpark stairway but was afflicted with 'brewer's droop'. Annie offered him her backside for $150 which he eagerly accepted (and prepaid for). Annie pulled the trick of making only her bum-cheeks available for his usage — but they heard someone coming to check the stairway. He hurried off while pulling his pants up, leaving Annie to her devices and his $150.

With such unsavoury encounters behind her, Annie had built up her database of mainly Caucasian regulars. One such was an airline pilot, another a married man who rarely had time for the full monty and would settle for handjobs in his car before rushing home in the evenings. Annie's people-skills of listening while sounding sympathetic worked well with Caucasian men. From two such clients, she's heard tales of how they'd married local Chinese women and came to wish they hadn't. One would complain of his argumentative wife who spent much in the shops and worked little in the house — and with whom he kept arguing over whether to give the maid every Sunday off or just the one a month. Annie also found that Caucasians could have a sense of humour about sex. Fortunately, otherwise one of them might not have seen the funny side of Annie answering her handphone while she was astride of him in apparently hot-sex action while telling the caller 'I'm busy right now, can I phone you back?'

Annie didn't splash her money on clothes and fancy things. She was buying up land and property back home in Vietnam. She also sent back money to her family, who thought her job in Singapore was doing the accounts for a restaurant group. Annie had set herself the overall target of $100,000 in savings, with which she reckoned could set herself up in a good business back home. Where she could safely draw a veil for the benefit of her family (and herself?) over how she'd really earned her start-up funding. There again, Annie so liked the Singapore results from her Japanese clients that when I last met her, she was pondering on how a working spell in Tokyo might pan out...

ORCHARD TOWERS PATROL
Christine's Story

*'I hire Chinese thugs for $500 to give a beating
to clients who cheat me.'*

Once at crowded weekends in Orchard Towers' Club
392, a girl had to act fast to close that sale. For the
female competition here was tough. Why, when I went
in its raucous heyday, before I'd even pushed my way
through to the bar at about 11.30 one Friday evening,
an amply-bosomed (I know, because she pressed them
flat against my chest) Thai temptress named Joy
greeted me by shaking a part of me that was not my
hand and spelt out her terms: 'I can give good f*ck, s*ck
and Thai massage, all night for $150. Can we go to
your room now?'

There was almost literally no space to move around
the bar area, and thus it was difficult to peel Joy off.
The loud (and bad) rock music from the band made
talking — or rather, listening — just as difficult. While
all around, flirty girls were catching my gaze and holding the eye contact that extra while longer, the way
working girls do. The (mainly Caucasian) male clientele was just as intent on getting, then drinking their
beer, as in succumbing to the allure of the usually Thai
siren calls being directed their way.

Two Singapore hookers sat on stools along the bar,
using this strategic position to help men to get their
beers (and claiming $1 each time as a tip for such as-
sistance), while at the same time looking disdainfully
around them at the 30-odd Thai girls who had not
come to Singapore just to improve their English.

Joy persisted with me, convinced that she had trapped her catch. Then suddenly a pal of hers caught her arm and shouted something in her ear. Joy backed away, and apologetically explained: her Thai friend had just phoned the bar manager of a nearby off-Orchard Road luxury hotel, and been given the OK. This meant that (so long as not more than six of them went) a batch of Club 392 girls could rush to that swish hotel bar, tip the manager his required $50 and hook up-market male punters there at a $300 minimum rate. It was a good racket and Joy rushed off, instantly forgetting about me.

I staggered out for a breather from the highly-charged human activity within, and got stamped on the back of my hand. To deter 'looking-only browsers', Club 392 operates a door policy of forcing a first-drink charge ($8 a beer).

And then, in the Orchard Towers entrance foyer, I encountered Christine. A Singaporean, Christine was a Eurasian whose family hailed from Malacca. And Christine was in a hurry. Not from a 'short-time' date but because she was late, having napped too long after her daytime job shift had finished.

Christine seemed relieved that she might not have to dive into Club 392, or indeed anywhere else in the night-time entertainment hub that is Orchard Towers. She preferred to try and conduct her business outside the bars or on the steps leading up from Orchard Road. 'There are so many Thai girls in Club 392. They're younger and prettier than me — sexy, too. And they're so bold! Sometimes, they try to steal your client while you're talking to him! They come up behind him and stroke his bum, then run their hand between the top of his legs through to his front. And then he stops talking with me...'

Plus, they undercut the standard unofficial Orchard Towers working girl's $200 minimum rate for all-night, and do a lot more $80 short-time business (which actually means as long as it takes for the man to 'do it', then clean up again — and skilled girls can trim the time taken to under 30 minutes). What's more, says Christine, Thai girls won't insist on the client using a condom if he refuses to wear one.

Christine won't go below $100 for short-times and besides, she doesn't really like the short-time style: 'Singapore is such a small place, so people who know me may see me at "work" earlier in the evening — and then talk about me. Late at night, that's not so bad.'

The sex-for-sale competition at Orchard Towers goes beyond the lower price ranges at Club 392 and Ginivy's. Upstairs, at the more upscale nightclubs, the really good-looking, dressed-to-kill, sex-bombshell Thai girls compete easily with the classier Singapore hookers and can get even up to $400 for a night with big-spending Caucasians (often American) or flashy local men.

And then there are at least four high-class escort agencies in Orchard Towers, busiest on weekend nights, where the charge is up to $200 per hour for escorting alone. Of which half goes to the (seriously attractive) girls — who can, of course, negotiate bigger bucks if they're prepared to entertain their clients beyond accompanying him to nightclubs, karaoke or restaurants.

So, in response to all this, Christine prefers to operate outside the building, where she can stop a man on his way in or out of the niteries — or do her business while sipping a *kopi* in the better-lit calm of the basement late-night hawker centre. She doesn't always succeed. In a good week, she'll get three all-nights. Sundays and Mondays, she doesn't even try. These are quiet nights, and the competition means the fewer men on the prowl can pick from a wider choice of available girls.

Now is Christine's second season on the game. She did it before, in 1988 when her (Malay) husband-to-be suggested that line of work as the easiest, quickest way of boosting funds for their wedding and subsequent married life.

'Business was good then, the Tropicana (on Scotts Road, where Pacific Plaza now stands) was in full swing and I could always get $300 for all-nights. There was plenty of men around then, looking for girls. Not so many now, because of Aids.'

Aids weighs on Christine's mind. She would walk out on a client if he refused to wear a condom. 'If I die, I want to die quickly, and not suffer a long-drawn-out death because of Aids. And all these Thai girls mean there's more Aids around.' And VD or other STDs would mean she had to take time off her night work.

That first time round, Christine worked for nearly a year before she got married. Now she's divorced, with a five-year-old daughter whom she sees on weekends, and she lives in Clementi HDB-land with family relatives who think she goes out nights to stay with her boyfriend.

Christine, a 29-year-old, has gone back on the game because of its obvious economic lure. 'I was working in a factory, sometimes doing 12-hour shifts, and on my feet all day. Now I'm doing canteen shifts, from 8 am to 6 pm — and I get $30 a day for that!'

So she's on her back all night many nights, and getting $200 for it. 'I'd try not to go cheaper than that, it's just not worth it to charge less. I take the risk, it's my body. Plus I insist on having Aids blood tests every two weeks, just in case. I go to private specialist clinics which don't report girls like me, but which charge $90 a test.'

When she started up her Orchard Towers patrol, she found she was out of practice and she had three bad experiences in her first two weeks. The first came when an Indian man hired her, then took her to a house where there was already another couple (the woman, a Filipina) and two teenage boys. Christine quickly decided she didn't like the look of it all — and what it could have led to — and she beat a hasty retreat.

The second was on a short-time session, using a typical Geylang small hotel. The man (a Chinese) sneaked out afterwards without leaving her any money, while she was bathing. She quickly dressed and rushed after him, but he'd disappeared. Exactly the same thing happened at a different Geylang hotel a few days later, this time with a Malay man.

So Christine changed her billing procedures. Now she demands money up front even before unhooking her dress. And the Malay man who cheated her probably still regrets it. For Christine learned through an

Orchard Towers colleague that the 'wild-looking' Chinese men who popped in and out of joints such as Club 392 and Ginivy's were in fact 'protectors' — not just pimps — for the Thai girls. That is, if there was any trouble with men that the girls can't handle, they'll step in — for a fee.

A good beating-up costs $500, which was what Christine paid when she spotted her Malay client at Orchard Towers again a couple of weeks later ('They always come back here, because it's where the girls are'). The Chinese 'protector' asked how badly she wanted him beaten up, and was told 'medium'. So, he went off, came back with five men — and they took the Malay out the back, to the dark corners around Hotel Negara. They informed him exactly why what was about to happen to him was going to happen to him — and set about rearranging his face.

Christine is not picky about her male clients, race-wise. 'I can't afford to be fussy! If I'm fussy, I die!' She has however found Chinese men to be the roughest, rudest and most blunt; 'but they usually prefer Chinese girls anyway.' It doesn't bother her either that virtually every local client is married: 'Men are like that, they'll always fool around.' She should know, that's why she left her own husband — 'he was a real butterfly'.

Christine now has a small list of six men who page her (or track her down at Orchard Towers), and whose preferences she has come to recognise. 'Some men want me to be excited, so I get excited. Other men don't care much about that, so I don't. I do whatever they want. They're paying, and the customer comes first!'

Yet, with a good man, Christine does enjoy her sex. She has a personal appetite for pleasures of the flesh which she dates back to her 'wild teenage years' in Clementi when she smoked, drank and 'did everything' with boys. But personal pleasures don't really matter to her now while she's at her night work. The (up-front) money is, of course, the thing.

Her ultimate ambition? Like many other working girls, Christine hopes to gather enough of a nest egg soon to go off the game and lead 'a normal settled life'. Besides, her current two-job double-life is physically tiring. Christine would ideally like to find that one man again with whom she can be just a housewife and mother, and nothing else. But that's what so many of them say, that's what so many of them hope for. The reality is unlikely to be so rose-tinted.

And Christine will probably find herself getting those night-time taxis from Clementi into Orchard Road for quite some while yet...

GEYLANG STREETWALKER (1)
Amy's Story

'If I need money, I come in here to work.
Simple, lah!'

Strange things can happen in Geylang. Especially to a man rambling by himself along its lorongs. It was on Lorong 16 that I saw a group of well-dressed flowing (mainly white) sari-clad, smiling Indian women heading my way. There were eight of them, ranging from a matriarchal Big Mama-type down to teenagers, all looking elegant, even stylish. I assumed they were a female family group on holiday here from India, and wandering around the areas near their budget hotel. I was wrong.

As we approached each other, one of the well-groomed younger women peeled off and came up to me. 'Give,' she said, 'give me money.' 'Hah?' I replied. Her friend — a more mature Singaporean Indian woman, it emerged — stepped in and explained that the girl was from India and couldn't speak much English. She added: 'That won't matter. She wants to make love to you. You want?' I demurred, so she switched tack: 'How about me, then? Enjoy! You'll like me!'

Her young friend was on offer at $150, herself at $100. We would go to a nearby Geylang hotel, she explained. As we parted, no deal done, I asked if those were 'white man rates'. The woman smiled, and said they were. Members of this group were obviously open to price haggling.

They all swept off down another lorong, taking up almost half the road space in width. Chinese men sitting outside the various brothels or pugilist arts shophouses smiled in mirth as the swirling saris swished past. I met them again, further down Geylang Road. Four of them were hailing a taxi. The cabbie asked where they wanted to go. They replied: 'Serangoon Plaza.' Off they went, another Geylang sideshow over...

Meanwhile, back on Geylang's small streetwalker L-shaped section formed by Lorong 14 and Talma Road, footballers were training on Geylang's pitch, men were idly watching their practice routines — and Amy was waiting for business.

She was waiting behind a brick wall with holes in it on Talma Road. By the gateway, two other women were more up-front. They were both Indonesians, over from Batam — and this was their patch. They didn't speak much English and only after their (unsuccessful) sales pitch, Amy stepped out onto the street to make her offer.

'I look at the man first, to see how he looks. If he's OK, I ask him if he wants to come inside with me. You? Can, lah!'

Amy is a Singaporean Chinese woman who's 25 but who looks much younger. She lives in Toa Payoh and was married at 18. She has one daughter, and her husband has been in prison twice for small-time ant-trafficking drug-related offences. The first time he came out, he was a changed man and was often violent with Amy. When he went inside for a second stretch, Amy put in for a divorce — and she's now on her own.

And often short of money. 'If I need money, I come in here to work. Simple, lah!' As she tries to be with her daughter as much as she can, Amy only does afternoon 'shifts' until early evening on as many days of the week as she needs to — or wants to. 'Not too much work in a week, too much f*cking is not good for me!' Though if overtime looks financially rewarding, she'll do it if she can make the required domestic rearrangements.

Her work 'uniforms' look tarty. One is a tight boob-tube on top without a bra (she has large breasts) and clingy, very short shorts. It pays to advertise? Or: 'Quick and easy to take it all off and put on again after,' as Amy explained helpfully. Working freelance, she averages three men per work shift, at the most four — though some days she has no customers at all.

She charges $50 for short-times and occasionally does weekend overnights (when a relative can look after her daughter) for at least $100. She delighted herself one night by hitting a jackpot — one night with a tourist in a plush Marina Square hotel for $200. It was a rare and unexpected treat that combined income and comfort.

For Amy's usual work is at the bottom market sector. 'I take all sorts — Chinese, Malay, Indian. It's OK if they can pay (she demands money first). Some men won't wear condoms; I know I'm clean but with them, I don't know how. I feel happy if they do wear a condom, and I always have one with me.' She goes for regular monthly sexual health checkups on her own initiative — 'Sometimes, I get worried…'

She enjoys doing sex with a 'good' man, she herself has a sexual appetite. But at this low end of the game, a girl cannot be over-picky as far as customers are concerned.

She has also had problems with the police. Amy is short (if well formed) and looks 17 or 18. And police cars regularly cruise this area slowly looking out for trouble — and for girls who should not be openly soliciting or even working at all here. On a few occasions, a police car has stopped and pulled Amy in. 'They think I'm underaged or Malaysian. They take me to the police station and I always cry. I don't have a Yellow Card so I show them my ID card, they see I'm 25 and Singaporean — and they let me go.'

Amy does most of her short-time work in a detached house adapted so that it can rent out its rooms for short lets (although, as it's well known to Anti-Vice police, the frequent unwelcome police checks are making Amy rethink the way and the place she does her work). Amy's house has eight spacious, clean rooms, all with a double bed and a shower unit. The charge per short-time (30 minutes, at the most) session is $10 for an air-con room, $6 for fan-only. Amy hints hard that she'd like a $10 tip on top of her 'professional fee', and she'll put in extra effort if such a bonus seems on the cards.

Amy's one of about a half-dozen semi-regular women who work this small patch during the afternoons. By nightfall, this figure has doubled — with the women (and an occasional *ah quah*) hanging around mainly on Lorong 14 (there's knocking shops on both sides of the mosque). They solicit likely looking men, with two women cutting costs even further by offering to conduct their services in the dark and thick scrubland over the other side of Guillemard Road.

These freelance streetwalkers are mostly mature women — Indian, Chinese and Malay — whose bodies, faces and coarse manners are telltale signs of a hard life — as you'd expect, for this is one tough way for a woman to make her living.

GEYLANG STREETWALKER (2)
Tina's story

*'Young girls f*ck rush-rush, and fake-fake'*

Tina has a problem, given her line of work. To put it, politely, she is not an immediately attractive woman. When I saw her heading my way along Geylang's Lorong 14, I feared she'd be like the ranting religious woman who'd stopped me on Geylang Road, just before I turned off into a wicked lorong.

Where it certainly wasn't my soul or a sin-free lifestyle Tina was interested in. She had placed herself in my way but seemed to want me to start any resulting conversation. I thought she might be a tout of sorts, who would ask me if I was looking for a 'nice, young, clean, sexy girl'. But no, it was Tina herself who wanted my business.

Rudely, I laughed a little but she joined in the joke. 'Yes, I know I look fierce. I look like a housewife, right or not? Some men are frightened to approach me!' She explained that her large and spectacularly non-designer spectacles were a necessity: 'I can't see men coming without these, and I can't tell if they look ones I want to approach. A woman on her own here has to be careful.'

We agreed on a *kopi-o*, and Tina was happy to tell me heaps more about herself. She was 33, looked older, divorced, one 13-year-old girl she supported by herself. They lived with her mother in Tampines but when Tina was at the 'office', she based herself in a cosy little room in a Lorong 14 boarding house. Outdoors, she worked a small well-defined patch between Lorongs 14 and 16.

Tina avoided the Indonesian area between Lorongs 12 and 10 and along Talma Road. She was wary of the frequent Anti-Vice police swoops on this patch that have thinned — though not removed — the ranks of 'awayday' Indonesian girls working freelance there. Indeed, in late 1994 two little hotels (thinly-disguised brothels staffed mainly by Indons) were forced to shut down, with one since being converted into a Bring Your Own short-term house ($10 for one hour, $15 two hours, $20 three hours and $30 all-night — 24-hour service), with the other wittily taking shape as nice yuppie flats.

Even though she's careful, Tina has been stopped on the streets and queried by police. But usually, when they saw she was Singaporean and Chinese (she kept her shoulder tattoos well concealed), they left her alone. She could look casual and indeed very like a sloppy housewife, and had got away with it sometimes by pleading 'I'm just waiting for my girlfriend'.

In-between patrolling and lingering, Tina rested at a nearby bus-stop shelter on Guillemard Road, an item of everyday street furniture that repays closer inspection.

At a quick glance, passers-by would simply assume this was a busy bus-stop, with an almost ever-present small gaggle of mature-looking women waiting patiently. Only all the buses come and go, and these women stay seated (if rarely talking of Michelangelo). Men who frequent Geylang may well take a seat in the shelter alongside such women, then open negotiations. Sometimes, the women are simply taking a break by taking the weight off their feet; other times, they drift off with their clients. I've watched this bus-stop a couple of times and rarely does a seated waiting woman get on board a stopping bus.

Tina had her own small band of regular clients who came looking for her and whom she took to her Lorong 14 room. If there were no regulars in sight and she needed the money, she would cagily pitch for new business by, if necessary, using the understated 'Looking for company?' line rather than the usual, explicit suggestions made by other streetwalkers. Tina's tariff rates were $50 for an in-and-out, plus $10 for the short-rent small hotel rooms along Lorong 16 she preferred. She wouldn't take new men to her own room, saying 'You can't be too careful — there's been murders around here in rooms like mine'.

Those men who did make it to her own room were in for a surprise. For a start, once she relaxed by removing those awful glasses and letting her hair fall down, she looked a lot less like a nagging wife and more like sexually attractive, if in an earthy way. And she enjoyed her sex...

She made a joke about the Year of the Dog, when I asked how she liked having her sex. Suspecting I was slow on the uptake, she explained she liked spreading herself on her front across her large bed and being approached from behind, doggie-style. But only when she felt completely relaxed and secure with a man. 'I must have the feeling. Then, I don't like to rush things. If he's big, I like a man to f*ck me strong. I'll shout "harder, harder". It makes my water come down.'

Tina first showered together with her men, making a discreet check on his sexual hygiene. Then, she didn't mind mouth-to-mouth kissing and she enjoyed giving oral sex if she was in the mood. She made her men wear condoms for every which direction he was approaching her from.

Her trusted visitors had more treats in store. Her room might be in a dingy bungalow but she'd made it homesy and well-appointed. Air-con, shower unit, big bed, supplies of chilled Red Bull energy drinks, strategically-placed large mirror — and a video. For this she had a small selection of frisky tapes she certainly didn't get from a local store. Two were soft porn, another two were pure porn (one featuring, I was told, unusual activities involving a male German Shepherd dog).

Tina liked to chat and she held strong opinions about her fellow streetwalkers. 'Thai girls are dirty, they don't make men wear condoms. Indonesian girls are dangerous to be near, they're always being arrested. And the young girls around here! They may be prettier than me but they don't know how to treat a man. They don't give him good service.

'They f*ck rush-rush and fake-fake, they pretend. But so many Chinese men only want young girls, and they don't care if it's quick if it's cheap and she makes him feel good. The men who see me want more than that, and they get more.' Why, Tina liked her regulars to spend a couple of hours with her.

A little while later, I went back looking for Tina. I was curious about that blue video collection and she'd promised to show me some highlights. Only Tina wasn't there, and the other women in her lodging house shouted: 'China woman, she go. She no come back.'

Outside, Stacey approached. She knew Tina well, and told me Tina wasn't going to be around any more but no, she didn't know (or wouldn't say) why. Stacey was another 30-something Chinese woman and, mistaking the nature of my Tina query, she pressed her own claim on me. She was in a good mood, having only just discovered the 'joys' of ang moh men. Her usual rate was the usual $50 but three nights before, a Caucasian man had paid her $200 and taken her to a nice hotel for the night. Because I seemed so pally with Tina, Stacey treated me almost as a friend and confided to me that the ang moh 'couldn't get it in'. Luckily, she said, she'd had some KY Jelly in her overnight bag.

Stacey said she lived in Johor Baru and didn't like coming to work in Geylang. But she had some bad mahjong debts (around $7,000) and her husband (who works in Singapore) often forced her onto the back of his motorcycle, dropping her off more frequently than she'd like in Geylang. She only worked daylight hours and got a lift back to JB on the motorbike. That way, she didn't encounter the male 'bullies' whom she said came out at nights. She knew the usefulness of that Guillemard Road bus-stop, and she used the same bedroom as Tina. Again, I declined her bold suggestions and she assumed it was simply because I preferred Tina. 'But I do ice cream better than her,' she implored.

I moved off and soon bumped into yet another mature Chinese woman, who was extremely direct. I told her I was looking for Tina. Insisting she knew all the streetwalkers on that strip, she asked suspiciously: 'Why?' I told her a story why, and she believed me. 'You won't find Tina, she won't be here for a long time. She's arrested for drugs.' Ah, so there was even more going on in Tina's little room than blue movies and well dodgy doggy activity! Little wonder then that she'd spent so many hours in there, rather than going out to solicit new business...

I was surprised, and fell silent for a few moments. Then this fat, crude and most unpleasant-looking woman saw her opportunity. 'How about me? I give you a good time. OK?'

'No thanks,' I said, too loudly, too quickly. As I turned around and wheeled off, I heard what I imagined were choice Hokkien obscenities directed at my retreating back...

THAI TAKEAWAY (1)
Patsa's Story

*'I like a man who makes
me feel many horny...'*

Patsa works in Ginivy's only, she won't go to other pubs. 'It's friendly in Ginivy's, and there's always many *farang* (Caucasian) men. I only go with white men now, they have good heart, they're kind, they treat me well, they're fun too.

'I avoid Singapore men; they talk-talk, look-look, and no money-money! They think they can get free f*ck! They look down on me, treat me like dirt. If they do offer money, it's only $50, sometimes even $30. Cannot! I want $200 for overnight, and $100 for short-time (usually an hour in a cheap Geylang hotel). It's not worth it, otherwise.

'And I read stories in the newspaper about girls being killed in hotel rooms — and it always seems to be Singapore men.' One case in particular she (as do other Thai working girls) recalls with a shudder. It was in December 1988, when a Thai 'businesswoman' — in Singapore for just a month — was found in a cheap Lorong 4 Geylang boarding house with her throat slashed and multiple stab wounds on her chest, sprawled across a blood-soaked bed.

In another similar case (August 1992), a 42-year-old Singaporean security guard met a Thai hooker in a Geylang Road music lounge, offered her $100 (she'd wanted $150) for sex, took her back to the condo block guardhouse in swish Leonie Hill Road where he worked, and had sex. But later, when she demanded another $50 for a second bout of sex, he attacked her. The fight got out of hand: she died, strangled by a lanyard. The guard originally faced the gallows on a murder rap but the charge was reduced to manslaughter — and in September 1993, he got six years' jail.

Thai Takeaway sex-for-sale girls in Singapore had to mentally take on board the grim if outside possibility of such savage male violence during the course of their work.

Also stung on a lesser charge, Patsa goes on: 'They try to steal too, take your jewellery, necklace and that. Once, with a Singapore man in my room, I went to the toilet but didn't bring my handbag with me. When I got back, the man had gone — and so had $200 from my purse!' So she tries to stick to *farangs* and for her that means Ginivy's.

Ginivy's, that doggone ole country and western pub within Orchard Towers' rear end, has long been a haunt for visiting and expat Caucasian men, especially oilies (oil industry workers, distinguished by their pot bellies which they like to rest on bar counters).

Ginivy's is also popular with visiting working girls, who group themselves inside this large pub for their nightly endeavours (pub hours: 8 pm–3 am) in national zones. That is, the Thai girls take one part, Indonesians (usually popping across from Batam) another, while visiting Malaysians have their patch — with the occasional Singaporean or Filipina picking her solo spot wherever it looks like she might 'close that sale'.

Patsa is an unofficial leader in the Thai section, as befits her age. She's 41, though she says she's only been hooking for four or so years. She spots likely male punters, makes much eye contact with them, always smiles or laughs, looks after the younger Thai girls new to the Singapore circuit (they usually speak little, if any, English).

Some of these girls (contrary to public belief) are seriously good-looking and certainly sexy-looking women — as are the Indonesians — but the mileage on Patsa's clock and her not-easy life mean she no longer possesses immediate 'shop-window' appeal. She makes up for it with her 'oomph' factor, her love of *sanuk* (all-purpose Thai word for 'fun') — and her popularity as a jive dance partner.

'I like to drink Guinness and I love to do Lock 'n' Loll,' she says — and she's very good at it as she ducks and swirls. This appeals to those Caucasian men roused by the driving if routine country and western music bands playing on stage.

Patsa first came to Singapore just over three years ago. Till then in Thailand, she had been a (by and large) dutiful wife but finally she decided she'd had enough of her husband's philandering, drinking and lack of money supply. 'With women, he was a butterfly,' she snorted. 'Bad man, no good for me.'

With a growing son to support by herself, plus ageing parents upland in northern Thailand, Patsa worked long hours in a Bangkok shop. Then a friend of hers, already on the game, told her about the rich pickings Singapore could offer for visiting girls willing to take off their panties and part their legs for money.

Taking a deep breath and clutching an English phrase book, Patsa headed south with her friend — and did indeed find that its streets were paved with, at least, more baht than she could ever earn 'honestly' at home.

She made a useful early conquest, a Dutch man involved with a shipping company. She moved into his Orchard Hotel room ('his company paid for both of us!'), and spent a comfortable three months there learning, among other things, enough English to conduct her business affairs. He's since gone home, though they still keep in touch through letters (that has to be all, he has a wife in Holland).

Patsa won't turn tricks for the Thai men working on Singapore's building sites. 'They remind me of my husband, they're like butterflies, and they might have VD or Aids.' But she does go to Golden Mile on Beach

Road for its Thai food, its money-sending services, to meet friends and chat. She won't work in Thailand itself, even though she has to return to Haadyai or Bangkok each time her two-week Singapore visit visa expires.

Patsa rents a room in Geylang for about $400 a month, but won't work in that area either. She says the Thai, Filipina, Indonesian women who do ply the lorongs, small hotels and bars of Geylang are 'dirty', and the men on the prowl there are not much better.

Business was better when she first came to Singapore. 'Then I had a man almost every night but now I can go through a whole week without one at all, once even not for two weeks! I think *farangs* have been scared off a bit by all that Aids talk, and they don't seem to have so much money to spend now.'

Patsa is convinced she can tell by a man's looks whether he's got a 'disease'. She does ask her customers to wear condoms (she always carries them herself) but if they object and they 'look clean', she won't insist. She tries to shower her men first; that way, she can check their dicks for visible clues as to their sexual health. She has regular health checkups during her many trips back to Thailand; she won't in Singapore as she doesn't want to appear on any computer databank.

Patsa will do most of the things a man may want, including blow-jobs. Besides, she likes sex; she enjoys doing it. 'I like making love with a good man. If he make me feel many horny, I'll be good to him. And make love three times to him overnight. I like the feel of good cock...'

As for the future, she has no immediate plans for retirement. Patsa would like to strike it rich, the way one of her Thai working girlfriends did. She met an elderly and rich Swiss man, and is now allegedly happily married and living in Switzerland.

There are no moral issues as such involved in prostitution for Patsa, only practical considerations (eg, will she be safe, can she trust him? etc). It's simple economics. From her Singapore earnings, she can see her son (now 14) through his Bangkok school and help her parents too.

Thai Takeaways do have a way of making a potential male customer feel he's contributing to an unofficial international aid programme when they tell him what they need his money for. But they're usually truthful, for these girls do not often splash their money on jewellery or designer clothes.

Patsa hopes male punters will continue to like her good grasp of English, her liveliness and her knack for 'Lock 'n' Loll' — at the expense of her better-looking, firmer-fleshed younger co-workers. And, for the while, her single hope is to get lucky like her girlfriend in Switzerland.

As Patsa, a true optimist, says with a wry smile, 'You never know...'

THAI TAKEAWAY (2)
Noi's Story

*'If they won't f*ck me, I could try Thai kick-boxing with them! Maybe they'd like that?'*

Singapore doesn't always work out for Thai working girls. After just four months, Noi decided she'd had enough. An attractive, almost petite 26-year-old from northeast Thailand, Noi had linked up with the Thai girls working the beat at a beer garden by Clifford Pier on Collyer Quay.

Each night from 9 onwards, the bar filled up with Thai girls. Before those 'witching hours', girls like Noi hung around their little Geylang base camp hotels. Noi's was on Lorong 24, the Singapore home for at least 20 Thai girls, sleeping six to a room if there were no overnight assignments elsewhere.

On the lorong's other side was an adapted terrace house with eight *cabines d'amour*: clean little cubicles, each with a shower unit and a huge bed taking up most of the space. Unless the Thai girls knew (or at least, trusted) their clients, they preferred to conduct their business in these Geylang cubicles (which charge $20 for short-term hire, $30 for longer, and $3 per condom).

And that was the problem for Noi. Her local (Chinese) boss kept her and her friends hard at it during the day, charging short-term customers $40 per session, of which $20 went to the girls. And they could each find themselves doing up to six men a day — before freshening up and lunging off for a hopefully more lucrative night shift at the beer garden.

If there was no luck there, it was back to that

cramped Geylang hotel bedroom. It was a daily routine that Noi decided she couldn't hack, despite her need for money and — be it said — her willingness to work. Even Thailand, she felt, was better than that.

The waterfront bar location meant it attracted seafaring men, the rougher sort. Plus the types the Thai girls dreaded — usually raucous, often drunk US Navy sailors on shore leave for whom the nightclubs of Orchard Towers were too pricey. 'They're so big, so crude,' muttered Noi. 'They say f*cking this, f*cking that. They won't pay much, they think they're in Pattaya — but this is Singapore, and it's so expensive here!'

Rather than argue with American sailors, Thai girls like Noi would simply not go to the beer garden whenever the US Navy was in town — giving the bar a rundown atmosphere even with its loud-loud-loud Filipino bands churning out the clapped-out rock classics.

Who the Thai girls were really hoping for — Caucasian men who pay well, often $200 per overnight, gave no trouble and didn't treat the girls 'like dirt' as Noi said local Chinese men did — didn't seem to find their way in big numbers to Clifford Pier. And a territory carve-up applied by local pimps meant that the bar's Thai Takeaways didn't ply their trade at Orchard Towers, and vice versa.

But back at their Geylang hotel, in the off-duty early evening hours before their night shift, the Thai girls could enjoy their *makan* and chat with each other — and it wasn't so miserable at all. Besides, the coffee shop just across the road had a Thai food stall, dishing out bowls of *tom yam* and other familiar whatnots. The girls could swop notes on what had taken place the night before, and what might await the night ahead.

One girl was making Noi and the others laugh their heads off. She'd just spent an overnight during which her male client hadn't made love to her once, he'd been so drunk and incapable. And she was almost hopping with frustration. For she enjoyed her sex, even in paid-for circumstances, and she was feeling frustrated. Another girl around the table in the hotel's little garden agreed — she didn't like it either, if she had no sex during an overnight.

So, the five girls held a straw poll on this topic of the moment. The vote went 4–1 against having no sex. The minority voter insisted that so long as he paid up, she'd be delighted to sleep out a night in a comfortable bed without having to do sex. Another girl grumbled, only part-jokingly, that not enough men chose her because 'I'm ugly'. It seemed to be the lack of making love that troubled her as much as the lack of income. She had a sudden idea: 'If they won't f*ck me, I could try Thai kick-boxing with them! Maybe they'd like that?' She stood up, and demonstrated some realistic-looking lunging kicks. The girls all broke out into gales of laughter, enjoying their brief daily period of *sanuk*.

But that wasn't enough for Noi. Too many girls in one bedroom had led to too many arguments over stupid little things. Too many unpleasant men, paying too little money during the day had depressed her. And hardly any Caucasian men during the evenings meant she probably wouldn't meet whom she was hoping to meet in Singapore: a *farang* who would take her away from all this.

So, Noi was happy she'd just got another job on a

one-year contract — working with the UN peacekeeping force in Phomn Penh, Cambodia, as a secretary/interpreter (her English was quite good). She had worked before with a UN battalion, along the Thai-Cambodia border area, and enjoyed it. It was good, regular, honest money. And if she needed more money, she could still 'throw a trick' now and then. After all, in 1992 the UN shipped in an urgent delivery to its men in Cambodia — half a million condoms.

What's more, said Noi, maybe a 'true romance' with a *farang* might come to pass for her in Phomn Penh — and then, at long last, she could tell a true story to her simple, rural Thai family about what she'd been doing with herself away from home — and how she'd be able to slip them some sorely needed money now and then.

Noi somewhat surprisingly came back to Singapore 18 month later. She'd made good money in Cambodia, and had even bought some land in Thailand. But she was still low on day-to-day funds and in the short term, saw few options other than returning to the familiar hooking scene.

This time around however, Noi was different. Now she was poised, well-dressed, more sophisticated — and with a new body-shape. She'd had her breasts noticeably enlarged with silicone implants, which she knew men would like the look of (if not the feel?). And now Noi was far more picky, with definite ideas on her preferred clients.

Initially though, her apparent poise only brought problems her way. She'd work Brannigan's and Top Ten mainly but soon realised she looked just too sophisticated and demure, not tarty and accessible enough. She'd sit there, rarely getting approached by men who assumed she was a tourist or had a boyfriend. Besides, most other Thai girls in these joints looked younger, sexier and had no trouble attracting business. Noi mused: 'I thought maybe I should wear a tight T-shirt, saying "For Rent"!'

Given that much is read and heard about how men regard working girls, I asked Noi for 'the view from here' — that is, how the girls themselves saw the men who came looking for their services. She gave me this highly-coloured, even strange, run-down on the preconceptions she and other Thai Takeaways had formed about male clients in Singapore.

• Not under 30: 'Too energetic, clumsy, no money.'

• Not Chinese: 'Too touch-touch, grope me everywhere and in public, they want cheap, they look down on Thai girls, think we're dirt. One wanted to f∗ck me quickly in his car. I told him "that's OK for your girlfriend but not for me, a hotel or nothing".'

• Not Japanese. Too 'strange'. Noi told me weird tales such as one involving seven Japanese men hiring a single Thai girl in Orchard Plaza Hotel, each paying her $250 and each taking his turn. Three hours later, the woman was richer but exhausted. Other tales she's heard of Japanese men involved dildos and the peculiar desire to 'study' a woman's private parts through a magnifying glass. Noi shuddered in distaste.

• Not German. 'They've usually had Thai girls before, they want everything and they pay only Thailand rates.

- Not Indian. 'They like to f*ck girls up the butt.'
- Not blacks: 'Too long, too thick, too painful. And they drink and swear a lot.'
- Not Thais: 'No money!'
- Not in Geylang, only around Orchard Road (where Thais tried to charge $150 for short-times and $300 for all-nights).

Which all meant that Noi tried to fish for who she thought looked the nicer kind of Caucasian man. Even so, her Singapore experiences second-time-round came over as a comedy of errors, almost like those old British farcical Carry On movies.

For example: Once in his ANA hotel room, her client suddenly started rolling his eyes, hyper-ventilating, rattling his tongue and making funny noises while she was giving him 'hand relief'. Noi panicked and just fled (without her fee), fearing he was having a heart attack.

In another hotel, her client asked her to cover him with bubble bath foam and then run her hands all over his body. She did and he came, almost instantly. She reacted by laughing aloud, which didn't please him much.

Another man wanted to be repeatedly smacked across the face, but again she spoiled it by giggling too much and not doing the smacking seriously enough for his liking.

Noi learned quickly to not be surprised (or laugh too much) whenever Caucasian men made odd requests of her, for which they paid handsomely ($300 and up). She also quickly learned how the current late-night Orchard Road scene worked. A fertile hunting ground was with the handful of other sophisticated-looking Thai women who post-midnight worked the stretch of Scotts Road between Marriott and Hyatt hotels, waiting openly around the underpass entrance near Scotts shopping centre or lingering in the half-shadows till they saw potential male clients coming their way.

Noi knew about the influx of Thai women into the Lorong 4–6 zone of Geylang but this time, she insisted on working freelance, only for herself and not for a boss.

Working freelance brought the usual headaches. Immigration authorities, mainly. At points of entry, such officials were demanding evidence of a return home ticket from single (attractive?) women coming here from around the region — especially Thailand, Philippines and Indonesia — plus visible evidence of spending money ($1,000 and up). Any doubt on these scores meant an entry refusal or a 3-day only tourist visa, which didn't give the working girls much working time here.

Once in Singapore, Noi's tactic became to use her apparent sophistication together with an affected look of vulnerability (despite those new breasts!) to attract the kindly sort of older Caucasian men who might take her under their wing — and their financial care. Perhaps even, given her language skills and intelligence, to employ her in some genuinely useful capacity in their businesses. For she liked the social scene in Singapore, especially the shops, the safety, clubs like Zouk and Studebaker's and the big-name pop concerts. She'd prefer to live and work here than in Bangkok, and she knows she has a lot to offer a 'good' man (she's also an excellent cook of Thai food).

Anyhow, Noi no longer possessed the right temperament, the patience nor the enthusiasm for the working life of the streets; that's a younger woman's game. If her big plan didn't work out, she had a fall-back position. She'd got enough money saved back home to rear a child and was looking for a suitable Caucasian man who could — with or without his knowledge/consent — make her pregnant and give her a baby (ideally, an 'elephant' boy) whom she would happily bring up by herself back in Thailand.

CHAPTER 4

Sex for Money, Money for Sex: A Fair Exchange?

The basic reason for prostitution is the same all around the world. It's a five-letter word, beginning with the letter 'm': money. Which makes prostitution not only the world's oldest profession, but probably also the world's most widespread female profession.

From the slums of Bombay's Falkland Road district (where some 8,000 women are packed into cramped brothels) to Europe's collapsed Eastern Bloc women (75 percent of the former communist world's unemployed people are female) who are flooding into the rich areas of western Europe, from the abandoned urchin teenagers of Brazil's major cities to the more upscale prostitutes in prosperous urban centres like New York, Los Angeles, Tokyo, Hamburg, Amsterdam, Sydney or Auckland.

Poverty and women's inability to earn a living in other ways may be the major motivating factors in why women around the world take to prostitution, but that's not the whole story. For sex-for-sale is as established in rich countries as it is in poor. Or in poor countries that become rich.

Prostitution exists whether it's First, Second, Third or worse Worlds. Whether it's voluntary or enforced. Whether it's for frills and treats, for fun and kicks — or for basic survival. Whether because it's the most obvious option for a woman, or because it's her only option. Whether it's legal, or not.

For as Time magazine noted in its June 1993 cover story Special Report on Sex For Sale around the world (Time provoked controversy by putting a Bangkok bargirl on this cover, though Thailand hardly figured in the news reports inside), prostitution is too often all a woman can do or — in many cases — the most obvious 'career choice'.

All this is a doomsday scenario which obviously does not apply to Singapore. For a start, Singapore is a successful modern economy with scarcely any of the real poverty found elsewhere in the region. It has a Women's Charter, which among other things means progressive policies towards women in employment, even if some (often, high-up) quarters still do feel that women should stay at home, look after their husbands and reproduce more often, etc.

Yet Singapore has its sex-for-sale, and this has some distinctive local characteristics. For Singapore's modern is intermeshed with its traditional Asian. Certainly as far as the relationship between men and women is concerned. For, by and large, the old Asian mindset of men as money-providers and women as money-receivers is still here.

Women earning perfectly good salaries of their own

expect their male dates to pick up the bills. Potential husbands are assessed by would-be mother-in-laws in terms of their financial status and earning potential. Potential brides get extremely excited at the prospect of a wealthy man, or one with the recognisable potential of accumulating material wealth.

Most young people, as the September 1993 Cost Review Committee Report found, want — make that, expect — the material good life. That is, they want landed property, bigger flats, cars and all that, and if they don't see that these ambitions are attainable, they feel 'frustration and angst'.

Singaporeans would thus appear to focus entirely upon the acquisition of things material, upon aspiring to what has got called a 'lifestyle'. If there are deeper and more meaningful values inspiring young Singaporeans, they're difficult to detect with the naked eye.

And so, today's young women wouldn't even think of 'marrying down'. They usually put financial security first, if asked to give a honest list of what they're looking for in their ideal life-partner — ahead of other qualities such as personality, companionship, sense of humour, emotional support, etc.

Now, women in hot pursuit of rich men for their husbands may be on different ends of the wavelength from prostitutes — but it can be argued that it's much the same wavelength, that the calculation made by both these groups of women when weighing up a man is strikingly similar in essence.

But, fortunately for mere hubby-hunters (as is not the case with prostitutes), the worst thing they're likely to be called by respectable society is 'gold-digger'.

Sex-for-sale in the region:
1, 2, 3: Snapshots of the sex trade in Thailand.
4: Haadyai, southern Thailand. A sexy floorshow at a typical nightclub.
5: Working girls at the sprawling 'Gang Dolly' area of Surabaya, Indonesia.
6: An advert selling a sexy show in Japan.
7: A topless bar in Auckland, New Zealand.
8: A sex-shop in Adelaide.
9: Peep-show in Tokyo.

This line of thought was put with more intellectual rigour (and depth) in a 1988 M.Soc.Sc thesis for the National University of Singapore, bluntly entitled Prostitution In Singapore and written by Connie Quah.

Among many other things, Ms Quah noted: 'While "normal" women attempt to use their sexuality via virginity, marriage and monogamy to gain material security, female prostitutes break through the social constraints of virginity, marriage and monogamy, and learn to exploit their sexuality to the fullest degree...

'In a sense, in terms of their social and sexual experience, prostitutes are very much like other women in general. For example, there are married women who also fake sexual pleasure just to please their husbands, because they feel they are obliged to provide sexual services for them. As one such woman told me:

"I have no feelings for my husband, but because he gives me $700 a month to support the family, I feel obligated to sleep with him."

'A prostitute may think that this is an even worse deal than what she herself is getting; the only advantage of being a married woman in this sense would be the absence of social stigmatization.

'Prostitutes are stigmatised only because they do not express their sexuality within the patriarchal institution of marriage...'

Indeed, love is rarely blind for many Singapore women — they carefully calculate the odds before letting themselves 'fall in love'. Somehow, Cupid's allegedly-random love arrows rarely pierce a Singaporean female heart if the handsome, virile man before them turns out to be a postman or bus-driver. But if he's rich,

Above: Sex-for-sale is a frequent cover story for major news magazines.
Below: In London, alluring cards like these are left in public phone-booths.

whether with money old, new or potential? Well, that's different, isn't it? Even if he's older and not technically available.

As a 25-year-old marketing executive named Peng told *GO* women's mag in early-1997: 'Older men know more about women and this makes them greater romantics and better lovers.' How's that, then? 'They have the money, they know how to give you a good time.' Oh, I see!

Peng's particular older man was 45, and a visiting-on-business Korean — with a wife and family back home in Seoul. And who had proved himself a 'better lover' by buying Peng virtually the full royal flush hand of 5Cs (including country club membership) that proves such an aphrodisiac for local material girls.

OK, so Peng told *GO* she occasionally wondered 'whether I'm just a little materialistic slut'. But she quickly pulled herself together as she recalled how 'he never says no to about anything and always indulges me'. Besides, as this practical-hearted lovebird concluded: 'Tomorrow, if he leaves me, I'll still have a condo, a car and a nice bank account...'

When *Her World* magazine (September 97) ran a story headlined 'Is a married lover a short-cut to the good life?' it attracted some intriguing reader responses. Such as 'Not Desperate' of Jurong East: 'So what if my companion is a balding, potbellied *ang moh*? If he is loaded and gives me lots of jewellery and money, and I in turn am a chic young thing for him to drape his arms around, why not? It is a symbiotic relationship. My morals aren't looser than the gold-digger who's trapped a sugar daddy of her own race into

In Macau: The Crazy Paris Show has been running for over 20 years.

In London: The Soho red-light district.

And in Amsterdam: Sex shops offering sadism and masochism (S n' M) as well as bondage and domination (B n' D) services.

marrying her.'

Sometimes, respectable Asian women can take great pleasure in what many men might regard as their lopsided view of married couples' financial arrangements. Such as this 27-year-old Hongkong accountant, who brashly told *Asia Magazine*: 'My money is my money; my husband's money is also my money.'

It was thus indeed significant that Singapore's Family Life education campaign identified this female mercenary mindset as a 'problem' in the new programme it launched in late 1993, under the slogan: 'Love Matters Most'.

For the central message in this Family Life campaign was different from its predecessors, which had urged sentiments like 'Spread a Little Happiness, If You Can' and 'It's Just an Introduction: The Rest is Up To You.'

Instead, the 'Love Matters Most' theme urged a 'realistic approach', stating: 'That's why it's so important to remember that it's not money or status that brings real happiness — but genuine, lasting love and companionship... Qualities that don't cost a cent, and can be found all around us — if only we care to look.'

And for their part, not all of today's men — it should be said — enjoy the too-typical female mercenary mindset. As a (male) feature writer with *The Straits Times'* Life! section put it in 1993: 'If women are angry that some men seem to see them as nothing more than sex objects, then men too should take offence at women seeing them as objects for money and security.'

Women as objects for sex; men as objects for money. The words were meant to refer to 'respectable' people

In Tokyo, sex-for-sale in all its many varieties is a commercial commodity much like any other. It doesn't provoke any blushes or raise many eyebrows, and it's difficult to avoid. It's there on hotel TV channels, along Shinjuku's sidestreets and in many public phone-booths.

— but it crisply states the context within which prostitutes and their male clients operate. And there're many Singapore women — hookers, mistresses, girlfriends, even wives — who would find the idea of sex 'for free' as downright strange.

As if they had no sexuality and no desire of their own, they would ask (as one woman did): 'Where got free f*ck?' And they would express surprise at the fact that so many Western women don't charge as they do it because they themselves enjoy doing it — or 'sex for its own sake'.

What would they make of modern Western woman as described by black US rap artiste Ice-T in men's magazine *Esquire*?

> 'Yo, listen up: They figured out the game.
> A '90s woman is out hawking sex just like you.
> You ain't playing her no more. She's playing you.
> She will f*ck you and not call you back.
> She'll tell you straight up, "I got what I want,
> now get out of my bed"...'

But in Singapore, when local newspapers and magazines try to deal with local female sexuality, the impression they often leave is of women as passive, as inactive, as nonsexual — and sometimes, as victims. The sub-text is that it's always men who are 'after it', while women just don't go in for 'that kind of thing' — not even those mature women, who were said in late-1993 to be victims of ageing but frisky Romeos at senior citizens' club folk-dancing and exercise groups sessions!

So, imagine the shock in early-1997 when *The New*

Above: Some may find it surprising that Israel has such an upfront sex-for-sale industry.

Right: Chile's capital city Santiago has several downtown coffee houses where the 'can see, cannot touch' waitresses are most vivid indeed.

Paper decided to splash all over its front page and two inside pages the vivid (if two-year-old) story of brainy 24-year-old Singaporean-Chinese student Annabel Chong, who had taken some intriguing detours during her academic pursuits in the US.

Annabel (wisely, not her real name) had in January 1995 won for herself a world record somewhat different in nature than the usual Singaporean fare of longest popiah, biggest mooncake, most Coke bottles, etc. For in Los Angeles, Annabel set a new high for the number of men with whom a single woman had enjoyed full sexual intercourse during a one-session sex orgy marathon.

During what was tagged The World's Biggest Gangbang, Annabel surpassed the previous record of 121 men in-a-row and was well on the way to her target figure of 300 when, after 10 hours of sex with a procession of 251 men (making a rate of one man per 2.4 minutes!), she gave up — an (understandably) exhausted woman.

At the time, this media sex event had achieved worldwide notoriety (with special I Was One Of The 300 T-shirts 'rewarding' the participating men) but was not reported in Singapore, except briefly in *ETC* magazine.

In January 1997, *The New Paper* made up for lost time. It quoted her as saying she was 'proud' of her outrageous world record, adding: 'People have called me a bimbo, slut and whore. But I just enjoy my body. I enjoy sex.' She explained that she had treated the gangbang as 'a sporting event' and had received 12,700 applications to take part from men around the world

Behold Annabel Chong, here getting the full tabloid front-page splash treatment in January 1997. Her unusual choice of extra-curriculum activities in the US shocked many Singaporeans.

— out of whom she'd selected those aged between 20 and 50.

Annabel also disclosed she'd been acting in American porno movies, appearing in 10 such videos since 1995 (having responded to a newspaper advert for porn actresses). She was at the time of the 1997 TNP interview studying for a Bachelor of Arts and Fine Arts degree in photography, gender and sexuality (well, it was at University of Southern California!) — and intended to undertake further research in, and lecture on, what she called sex studies.

The New Paper filled in her Singapore background details, giving her real name, where she was brought up (in Changi), the high marks she'd won in all school GCE exams, and quotes from ex-schoolmates who described the teenaged Annabel as 'wholesome, quiet and talented'. It also gave the comparatively calm response of her parents to what their only child was doing ECA-wise in the US, and disclosed that she visited her home here every year during university vacations.

TNP readers inevitably responded in their droves, usually registering 'shame, shock, pain, disgust'. One reader slammed the paper for printing Annabel's photos: 'You are destroying whatever little is left of girl's dignity, worsening her parents' already sad predicament.'

The New Paper editor felt obliged to print reasons why the paper had thus splashed the Annabel Chong story, such as 'with more Singaporeans sending their children to study overseas, Annabel's story would be a timely reminder of the dangers.'

Strangely, it emerged that the particular target for

In Australia (above) and the UK (left), sex-for-sale in its various forms can take on the full frontal approach as seen in these men's magazines.

TNP readers was the reporter who had interviewed Annabel in Los Angeles and written up the story — with 80 per cent of Internet postings on the topic not being anti-Annabel as such but slamming the (female) reporter. The newspaper responded with the 'don't shoot me, I'm only the messenger' line of defence.

Clearly, the story of Annabel Chong hardly squared with most Singaporeans' preferred image of their young womanhood...

Back home again, in July 1995, when a man (accused of raping a woman clerk and forcing her to have oral sex with him) told the court that in fact she had initiated their 'friendly' sexual encounter, great surprise was expressed. The DPP reportedly displayed disbelief because the defendant was claiming that the woman had actually been 'the initiator, the prime mover'! He said that other witnesses had described the 22-year-old clerk as 'timid' and 'quiet'.

The issue of oral sex, arising from this rape court case, became a Singaporean legal matter by itself. The original ruling was that oral sex did not fall within this Penal Code definition of unnatural sex (section 377): 'Whoever voluntarily has carnal intercourse against the order of nature with any man, woman or animals shall be punished with...'

However, in February 1997, Appeal Court judges ruled that oral sex was only 'natural' as foreplay to conventional sexual intercourse between a man and a woman — and that 'natural sex' involved 'the coitus of the male and female sex organs'. Outside this strict context, oral sex was ruled 'unnatural' and therefore illegal.

One side-effect of shaking off communism's chains was an upsurge in Prague's sex industry, which now takes on a variety of forms. This troubles many Czechs, who suspect that Russian mafia gangs control most of the city's sex rackets. Major customers are German men, lured across the neighbouring Czech border by the much-lower sex-for-sale prices charged by obliging women from various parts of ex-Soviet bloc eastern Europe.

Justice Karthigesu commented: 'It is a fact of life, in humans as well as animals, that before the act of copulation takes place, there is foreplay to stimulate the sex urge. Kissing is the most common, although there are several others.' Noting that statistics showed that oral sex was widely practised in Singapore, he added: 'We cannot close our minds to that.'

Actually, the most recent (known) research into this topic was conducted in 1982 by Dr Aputharajah for his Sexual Behaviour of Women in Singapore book. He said that nearly half (42.9 per cent) of the 1,012 local women (aged 20–34, all races/religions) he surveyed had practised or were practising oral sex. He specified that 35.8 per cent of the unmarried women and 43.7 per cent of the married women he had interviewed said they had engaged in oral sex.

Dr Aputharajah added that the women were the ones who mainly performed the oral sex — and not the other way round. He observed: 'The wide acceptance of orogenital (oral sex) activity is remarkable as it was considered a perversion only a generation ago.'

But back to that local sexual climate, which seems to be almost a throwback to the 1950s' western world maxim before sex was 'invented' in 1963: Nice girls didn't, bad girls did. And almost as if in Singapore, one class of (lower-educated) women cater for men's urges while the other (better-educated) class hold out for that wedding ring and respectability with their own desire well in check, if in existence at all.

Plus, a prevalent national creed in today's Singapore is materialism. That is, pretty much everything judged in terms of its price, of how much, of what discount, of clipped coupons, of buy one get one free, of free gift or not, or lucky draws, of puerile contests, etc. It's a materialism that also determines charm, courtesy and other such basic human virtues — which in other communities are displayed and given freely and naturally.

And so, there are more than 6,000 women selling sex in Singapore. And so what? For are 'respectable' Singaporeans — especially women — truly fit to sit in moral judgement on prostitutes?

Why, it could almost be argued that such women can continue being prim and respectable because there are so many other women who voluntarily hire out temporary access to their own bodies for those men who otherwise might get mighty irked at — and mighty impatient with — how respectable these respectable women think they are.

Already, to my certain knowledge, there are many single men (local and expat) in Singapore who are reluctant to go near 'nice' women at all. The easiness of a misunderstanding that results in an accusation of 'molest!', the difficulty in disproving such charges or the pointlessness in suggesting that the woman was, at least initially, a perfectly-willing partner in flirtation — and the grim legal penalties of a molest/modesty-outrage conviction (up to two years in prison or heavy fine or caning, or any two of these punishments).

Indeed, a male letter-writer to *The Straits Times* in 1996 called for the molest law to be revised. As he put it: 'As it now stands, men are the disadvantaged gender and this vulnerability makes them easy targets, especially for those who possess ulterior motives. All a woman has to do is to make the accusations and the law takes its course. In the course of defending himself, the man is poorer, his integrity is shaken, his family affected and at the end of it all, his life will never be the same again. Is this fair to male citizens?'

These all add up to real reasons why many men turn to 'professionals' for that kind of thing — and keep physically well clear of 'nice' women, even in recognised girl-meets-boy joints and even if such women's exciting styles of dressing suggest at least some sort of interest in male reactions.

Local men have been quoted (in *Her World* magazine) as saying they won't get into a public lift if there's a woman alone already there — for an almost-paranoid fear she might scream 'molest!' Another man reportedly found himself locked up for a couple of days after an alleged molest on a crowded MRT train, when he insisted he was unwillingly pushed up against the woman by people pushing him from behind.

It's clearly an unhealthy and immature state of affairs, with both sexes at fault. Some women argue it's good that men are 'running scared' and that 'now they know what it's like to be afraid'. And no-one could defend those grown-up but sexually-immature — even, mentally sick or downright deviant — men who point torches into cars at courting couples, who drill holes in women's cubicle doors for a weird peep show or who (with the aid of a mirror) point video cameras up women's skirts and such like.

There are, of course, many modern men in Singapore who are perfectly well-adjusted — and often well-travelled, and thus aware of how more sexually-mature women conduct themselves elsewhere. It's some of such modern men — not inepts, weirdos or mother's boys — who are choosing to avail themselves to the many sex-for-sale women working in Singapore, thereby avoiding that dreaded word 'molest'.

And the response of such men when and if women criticise them for such sexual behaviour is often: 'Mind your own business!'

Besides, often the only means through which women workers in the commercial sex industry can climb up to claim their place on board this 'ship of fools' that is this modern materialism, is by selling what they might otherwise just be sitting on. Who would deny them their right to get thus on board? Respectable women, who married 'well'?

For sex-for-sale is just another commodity, one among many, in today's lucky-draw, free-gift, door-gift, table-gift, what-prize, what-price, got-discount, want-want-want, me-first, me-only, me-now, money-mad, materialistic Singapore.

Men want sex, women got it. Men got money, women want it. Wife, girlfriend, mistress — or prostitute. Simple, isn't it? And yes, it is thoroughly primitive, isn't it? But that sure is the way it is.

The Battle Against Aids

It was in 1985 that Singapore recorded its first case of sexually-transmitted HIV, the virus that usually leads to Aids. The victim was a Singaporean male homosexual. By 1990, 57 Singaporeans were confirmed HIV-positive. In 1992, this figure stood at 178 — of whom 53 had developed Aids (42 of these had died from the disease).

A Health Ministry official then observed: 'The trend shows that commercial sex is now the most common mode of HIV transmission among Singaporeans.' For a 1991 survey had found that between 30 and 40% of men visiting prostitutes did not use condoms, did not want to — and were not asked to do so by the women.

So in May 1992, Project Protect was launched pitched primarily at prostitutes and their clients. Its 'use condoms' message was reinforced at Kelantan Lane's DSC Clinic which prostitutes had to visit for regular sexual health check-ups.

By end-1996, Dr Roy Chan (on behalf of Action for

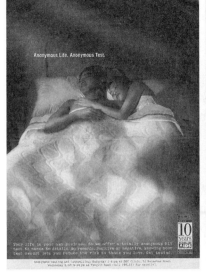

In mid-1998, Action for Aids launched eye-catching adverts (above) for secret HIV testing at Kelantan Lane's DSC Clinic. Meanwhile, government adverts (right) delivered the 'No Casual Sex' message — even at bus interchanges (below, right). Too late for that in cathouse bathrooms (below), where Project Protect is more the point!

Aids Singapore) noted: 'We are fortunate in Singapore to have an enlightened approach to disease control among brothel-based prostitutes. The transmisison of HIV in local brothels is now almost zero, thanks to the medical screening and treatment of sexually-transmitted diseases and an aggressive effort to increase condom use to 100%.

'I believe that we have been spared an Aids epidemic of the proportions in Thailand and India mainly because of these interventions, much less the result of mass media campaigns stressing monogamy and abstinence.'

By early-1998, the HIV-positive figure stood at 694. Of these, 235 had died from full-blown Aids while another 121 were confirmed Aids victims. A 1997 breakdown found that 428 victims were hetereosexual, 109 homosexual, 72 bisexual and 22 others (drug users, etc) — with the oldest known HIV-positive male being 75 years of age. Like most other older-generation HIV victims, he'd contracted the disease from visiting prostitutes overseas, which explained why Health Ministry posters appeared at Changi airport and WTC's Indonesian islands ferry terminal urging: 'Aids. Be Safe. Not Sorry.'

A Road with a Past

Malay Street today is a sweetly restored shophouse row embodied within the air-con, covered-over bosom of the modern Bugis Junction complex. Dainty little gift stalls, swish boutiques and designer stores line its sides. Often lured by its shopping-in-comfort are Japanese office lady tourists.

Time was when the Japanese women at Malay Street were known as Karayuki-san — only it was them providing the 'comfort' available here, and what was on sale there were not tasteful yuppie knick-knacks. For until the early 1930s, Malay Street was the very centre of Singapore's sex-for-sale scene. And there, hundreds of far-from-home Japanese whores based themselves — and braced themselves — to take on all comers.

As British journalist Bruce Lockhart wrote about the 1910s' Malay Street, it had 'long rows of Japanese brothels with their lower windows shuttered with bamboo poles behind which sat the waiting "odalisques" (ie, the girls), discreetly visible, magnificent in elaborate headdress and brightly-coloured kimonos, heavily painted and powdered, essentially doll-like and yet, not without a certain charm.'

Other women worked here, too. Lockhart again: 'Malay Street was where the white wrecks of European womanhood and young Japanese girls, silent, immobile and passionless, traded their bodies for the silver dollars of Malaya.'

Lockhart recalled a Madame Blanche and her 'collection of Hungarians, Poles and Russian Jewesses — a frail army of white women recruited by professional pimps from the poorest populations of central and eastern Europe, and drifting farther East as their charms declined, via Bucharest, Athens and Cairo, until they reached the "ultima Thrule" of their profession in Singapore.

'Sometimes a Malay princeling or Chinese "towkay" would make his way discreetly to this sordid temple (ie, Malay Street) in order to satisfy an exotic and perhaps politically-perverted desires for the embraces of the forbidden white woman.'

If Malay Street sounded fun in a raucous way, it wasn't. Another observer wrote of it: 'Here, you could be beaten up and robbed for 50 cents, or knifed for a dollar.'

These days, the worst robbery that can hit Malay Street visitors is a fine imposed for breaking its no-smoking rule. And of course all traces of vice are long, long gone. No, there's nothing at today's dinky Malay Street to inform visitors of its definitely dodgy sex-for-sale past.

Singapore's Theme Park Brothel

When Jurong's Tang Dynasty City opened in January 1992, its recreation of an ancient China brothel called Chamber of 1,000 Pleasures caused much excitement. In it, five brightly made-up local Chinese beauties served as 'concubines', waving their scarves at guests and posing for photos with them.

But it didn't last long. It seems that some (male) visitors thought the theme park bordello was for real, and that the girls were offering genuine 'services'. In their turn, the girls complained bitterly at this male confusion between real and pretend life...

The Chamber of 1,000 Pleasures is still there, but without its lovely concubines.

Inside, the 'bordello' is a visual delight with flowing pink bed-curtains, ornate wooden beds and charming clothes as worn by such consorts (who also then recited poetry and played music) in the Tang Dynasty era (618–907 AD).

At Singapore's other major theme park Haw Par Villa, prostitution also gets a look in — but with a rather different message. For in HPV's justly-famous (and terrifying) Ten Courts of Hell, the Second Court sits in judgement on those guilty of robbery, inflicting physical injury, gambling — and prostitution. The statutory punishment for transgressors? Being drowned in pools of blood, and filthy blood at that!

Actually, it could be even worse in these Hell Courts' gore-filled torture chambers. Business fraudsters, tax dodgers and those showing lack of filial piety get their bodies ground between two large stones, while loan-sharks are thrown onto a hill of knives and those swearing or wasting food have their bodies sawn in half. Cheating in exams? Intestines pulled out!